Texas West of the Pecos

Bindweed heliotrope on shifting Pecos dunes.

Stormy sundown over the salt flats.

Texas West of the Pecos

Photographs and text by

JIM BONES, JR.

TEXAS A&M UNIVERSITY PRESS

COLLEGE STATION

Copyright © 1981 by Jim Bones, Jr.
All rights reserved

Manufactured in the United States of America
FIRST EDITION

*This is for my family, with whom I first saw this desert,
and for all who have opened their hearts and land to me.*

Contents

Introduction

Texas west of the Pecos is a solitary region, mostly uninhabited, empty space, widely defined by the Rio Pecos, Rio Grande, and New Mexico state line. With Langtry, Orla, and El Paso at extremes, it embraces more than thirty thousand square miles of wildly varied land bound together by the drainage of its streams.

Human history gathered here like a seasonal storm, raged for a moment, then largely disappeared, leaving only a trace of impoverished soil. Early paleolithic people may have crossed the Trans-Pecos a hundred thousand years ago, but if so, they saw a very different world. At the close of the Pleistocene epoch about ten thousand years back, before the Chihuahuan Desert succeeded, Rocky Mountains woodlands interspersed with arid species covered West Texas, right down to the banks of the old Rio Grande, in a way unlike anything that can be seen today.

About six thousand to eight thousand years ago when the region began to warm into savanna grasslands, new waves of humanity swept in, drove immense herds of mammoth creatures to extinction, and then ironically followed, themselves. Some observant tribes, however, learned to gather wild plants to supplement game and in time became cultivators of domestic crops along interior rivers.

Spanish explorers in the sixteenth century first charted this part of Terra Incognita as El Despoblado and went weeks out of their way to avoid its desolate heart. The Río Conchos was their first corridor of incursion, but guided by native slaves, the Spanish struck out cross-country from Chihuahua for the Rio Grande and Santa Fe. Apaches and Comanches had their own violent way for three hundred years. Then nineteenth-century European settlers, soldiers, and fast-deal promoters arrived in force, killed off the buffalo, extinguished the early immigrant races, and in one generation, with windmills, livestock, barbed wire, and railroads, effectively converted open ranges into splendid arid wastes.

People now living came to West Texas at the turn of this century for frontier land, for then it was a legendary place to get a whole lot of nothing for not much money and to take what could be forced from the rest. Empires, too big to ride across in days of hard travel, grew on foreclosed dreams. Elbow room was always plentiful, and in places, at first, so was rich forage. Some settlers had knowledge to complement desire and wisely managed their natural trusts, but most who started with good intentions and the myth of unlimited frontier ended up droughty, beaten down to dust. Their herds were seldom still, and razor hooves cut ruts that swelled and spilled the real earthly wealth back into rivers and the sea.

Many drifters also searched for mineral wealth. A few got rich. Most died busted. In its heyday, quicksilver was king along the cinnabar belt from Lajitas and Terlingua to Study Butte and Mariscal Mine, but Shafter produced hard silver. Easy ore played out early, though, and since World War II the silent pits that drop out of sight a stone's throw from abandoned shacks and neglected graveyards have yielded little. During big booms, local folks tried to grow cotton and food, but long droughts left farmers out of luck, bottomlands depleted, and villages like Terlingua Abaja melting back into dirt. Traditionally, in our closest relations with land we have tended to plunder and punt, get while we can and move on to new options, but in the long run there never has been a real frontier of unexploited riches, and now the grim reaper of geometric population growth has outstripped every scheme, leaving us all caught up by faster feedback than we can handle.

Long mistreated, this empty waste is not easy country to know—neither the intricately dissected mountains, where to go a straight map mile on foot can take a whole day of up-and-down bushwhacking between house-sized boulders and over ridge tops worn sharp by wind and invisible water, nor the flat, desolate plains around ranges, where without air-conditioned automobiles the ignorant can perish in just a few hours. Impassively the desert stabs, strikes, grabs, tears, claws, bites, stings, throws you down, and lifts you unexpectedly. It smells sublime after rains and parches with thirst unequaled. Its heat can make heads pound so hard no work is possible or kill the arrogant with hardly a stroke. Just surviving requires about a gallon of water a day, even in the shade, in the furnace months of summer. The muddy river offers no ultimate relief, for it can rise fifty feet overnight or spread a mile wide, all without warning, even under cloudless skies, from rains out of sight upstream. Just the same, you cannot sit at home and dream of how you feel about this land. If you really want to know, you have to be here, silent and open to voices that speak of time and space with curves continuous, of hands and leaves, of stones and paws, of water like jade and the stars, and of how all are joined at infinity.

If it were possible to approach this wide country again, for the very first time, in some logical order, I might begin at the confluence of the Rio Pecos and the Rio Grande where the land slopes gently up from the wetter Edwards Plateau and Lower Valley. I would sweep north over dry plains to the Guadalupe Mountains, west across to El Paso, south down the Great River to the Big Bend, swing often into ranges that rise nearby, and then drift slowly eastward through deep canyons back to the place where I started.

To truly know the region, I would also have to journey far beyond, into the lush Mexican headwaters of the Sierra Madre where the Río Conchos is born and to the peaks of the San Juan Mountains of Colorado where the Río Bravo del Norte rises as alpine freshets, and then cascade with ocean roots from the continental divide to the Gulf of Mexico. But by chance of fate, we seldom get such wishes.

As an adolescent, I crossed the Trans-Pecos with my mother, Nell, father, Jim, and young brother, Robert, while moving from Norfolk, Virginia, to Vandenberg Missile Base in California. The Despoblado seemed to me then only a curious land of mineral treasures and stark peaks, empty of the powerlines, roads, and buildings that crowded eastern horizons.

I remember looking out for hours, forehead against the car window, at desert and dusty towns that grew without much shade. From a highway bridge over the Pecos River I briefly saw daring young couples swimming nude in clear water. The gents grinned broadly, showing off, but one woman was too shy to take off her slip, and the other turned modestly away. We crossed the edge of pink dunes that rolled, rounded, Venus-mounded, in the pale twilight and passed gas flares that danced while pounding pumpjacks sucked at tarry fossils buried miles beneath the sand.

At a roadside stop Robert and I walked away from the cramped auto into wide-open spaces. Sheep grazed up against a fence like woolly thistles while woody tumbleweeds danced over the broken ground, and my little brother turned uneasy, then ran downwind, chased by a plant taller than himself. Tumbleweeds, those popular symbols of the Old West, paragons of freedom and independence, that roam nearly everywhere unopposed, are actually Russian thistles. Silent intruders, brought in with livestock feed from the steppes of Central Asia, they spanned the Great Plains in just twenty years, all the way from Alberta in Canada to the Gulf of Mexico.. Bermuda grass, giant cane, salt cedar, and even bullfrogs are similar biological invaders.

Five years later, as a college freshman I rolled not through but into the Despoblado. From Austin I went west to Marfa and then south to Presidio, crossed the border at Ojinaga, and entered the Sierra de la Parra with graduate students and my early geology teacher, Bill Muehlberger, who later trained astronauts to collect moon rocks. We left paved roads and most signs of human habitation right away, but trailed white plumes that marked our routes in chalky dust.

The lean desert was relentless in immensity, inscrutable in origin and form. I saw unimaginably wild country and learned things that forever stretched my ideas of life and nature beyond the old mold. My most significant discovery was that experts are exactly as human and fallible as the rest of us. Geologic knowledge, it turned out, is not absolute. I went looking for changeless foundations and instead found continual change. I also learned Western Arm Waving, guarded secret of Despoblado geologists. Everyone, it turns out, is entitled to stand on an outcrop, look perceptively about, point, shout, jump around if necessary, arms waving, and elucidate educated uncertainties, with theories for the impossible jumble of mountains and valleys that stretches in every direction.

My companions were elated to be back in the desert. I was overwhelmed. My skin cracked, needles stuck me, and the sun forced me into shadows at noon. I thought it inconceivable for anyone to really love that hard country, unaware it had gotten through my tender hide and had quietly seized my heart.

We traveled roads that showed only as hand-drawn lines on homemade maps, searched for cephalopods to place conjectured events, and examined huge structures that showed that folding mountains once slid over gypsum into basins below. Above, huge blocks of petrified seabed broke into mile-high waves that rolled to the horizon beyond the ash and rubble of extinct volcanos.

We were greeted peacefully at scattered rancherias, offered breakfast with yucca blossoms by a child at one, and were always asked where to dig for water. Not oil or gas or gold, but water. Answers were difficult and given with care to avoid sending anyone on a wild, desperate chase. By lying on our bellies in the chaparral and leaning over an abyss, we had seen the dry fruit of hard labor—a fifty-foot shaft, hand-dug, where no water could be found.

Nearly dry ourselves, we stopped at a well in the mouth of an empty wash before climbing over the mountains and immediately noticed a funny odor in the air. Floating at the bottom, surrounded by flies, was a dead coyote, eyes wide

open, lips curled back, thick tongue clenched by sharp teeth. Driven mad by thirst and the smell of water, it had attempted the impossible and paradoxically drowned in the desert.

We quickly ground through the arroyo, skirted a canyon wall, and topped the pass. While the others wrangled in the sun over redrawn maps, I wandered away to crouch in the shade. From a dark, weathered ledge, perfect casts of ancient urchins projected, etched by rain, wind, and sand raised slowly from a dead sea. Half a mile below, wavering dust devils danced up the bolson floor, wind rattled ocotillo at my head, and for an instant I vanished. I did not lose consciousness; on the contrary, I became minutely aware of everything around me, immersed in clear desert light. Then the carryalls started, and I was wrenched back to my place on the gear. We rolled on for hours through the bright, monotonous land toward the river and civilized streets, but the world never appeared the same to me again.

Big Bend National Park

In 1909, J. O. Langford started south out of Alpine with his pregnant wife and first daughter, heading sight unseen for a homestead on the Rio Grande that promised hot springs and a healthy new life away from malaria and cities. They were captivated by wild animals, beautiful landscapes, and tall grasses sprinkled with flowers. Fours years later when border troubles erupted, soldiers came in to patrol, and all settlers were evacuated.

By the time the Langfords returned in 1927, their new homeland had changed dramatically. Reacting during World War I to demands for protein, and the promise of profits too big to pass over, ranchers crowded stock onto relict ranges, and in places where stockmen now reckon sections to the animal, there were at times dozens of head to the acre. That kind of bonanza did not last long. It was too much like mineral wealth, a one-shot affair, with only enough to make a few rich quickly at the long expense of the future.

After going home, J. O. Langford said: "Where once I'd thought there was more grass than could ever be eaten off, I found no grass at all. Just the bare, rain eroded ground. And where once beautiful pools of clear, cold water had stood in Tornillo Creek, now I found only great bars of sun baked sand and gravel . . . and never again did we have that which we'd had in the beginning. Somehow, a brightness seemed gone from the land."

A few farsighted individuals realized the greater potential in limiting herds to sustained carrying capacity, but the prehistoric affluence of the plains was eaten to the ground anyway. Thousands of years may be needed to build an inch of this arid soil. It takes rain falling, acids dissolving, and tiny organisms patiently digesting raw minerals and then laying down their bodies with dead plants to make fertile the naked earth. Silurian land life found only bare rock to colonize, and our small mammal ancestors lurked in jungle shadows until millions of years ago when Miocene grasses flourished and spread grain over the world. Vegetation continues to profoundly influence animals and climates as the humble net of roots, stems, and leaves that is the weedlot, prairie, and alpine tundra holds water in the soil and shades the surface of the earth.

The ubiquitous dark evergreen shrub commonly called creosote bush quietly takes over the desert with brittle gray branches, small, hard leaves, yellow flowers, and fuzzy seeds. It bears the lovely botanical name *Larrea* and fills the air with fragrance after rains. Widely spaced, in places it can be the only thing alive between bare rock and sky, and then it reassures even the internal observer that somehow Nature can endure the harshest of hardships and survive.

However, hard times are nothing new. The geologic record shows several worldwide constrictions of life in our planet's history, but Nature's ace is diversity to counter the enormous attrition of life precariously feeding on itself at the breaking edge of extinction. Physical life is here and now. There is no endless reservoir out of which it arises other than its own lonely self, moment to uncertain moment. So it has been since cells first replicated in nurturing seas, a billion or more years ago: no guarantees, but definite seasons to bank on and cycles of restoration and rebirth. Humans have broken that faith and threaten to cut threads that go back to the very beginning of life. Once severed, those threads can never be rejoined.

Looking for my first desert photographs, I went to J. O. Langford's hot springs with my former wife, Ann Matlock, at Thanksgiving one year. We walked up Tornillo Creek through jagged Boquillas flagstones and found only dry gravel coated with salt by dying pools. I turned down along the river to the blasted bath house, but it, too, was invisible under a flood blanket of fine mud washed in from the old ranges. Water trickled over bright pebbles where the hot springs lay temporarily buried, and a steady line of pilgrims toured the defunct spa, dipped their hands, and shook their heads in wonder. I fell into shallow water, sank to the bottom, and wallowed into the muddy bed of uplands drifting to the sea. Roaring currents washed me, and, buried to my chin, I became the endless river, filling oceans with mountains to someday stir again. Sunshine buzzed in willow thickets, catfish glided by, and sand washed downstream while I was left behind, a possible fossil, inert until the next rise.

On the west side of the park we went across the Rio Grande at the mouth of Santa Elena Canyon for a close look at Spanish goats that browsed the steep cliffs. Their golden eyes narrowed as we approached, then tough *hombres y mujeres*, with no-nonsense ways, quickly led *los niños* up tumbled rocks with grace and ease, well beyond our reach.

At low water we walked several miles into the canyon along sandy banks, fording often at shallow rapids and riffles, and cliff swallows were startled to see us peer into their pot-bellied nests, normally protected by the riverine moats. We rested at midday under a boulder by green Mexican persimmons, then toward evening, when the heat let up, we both floated out, surrounded by turtles who waited for stray birds to fall.

Determined to do it all the first trip, we drove to the middle of the park and climbed into the Chisos Mountain Basin for a cool alpine snooze. All night, however, raccoons contended with arachnids and skunks for campground scraps, and at breakfast javelinas snorted crudely through, but the Window view was worth it all the same.

Most people have an origin myth, whether they are drawn from an ancient ocean broth or the hand of a wrathful god. At the Dawning, according to the Apache Indians, the Great Spirits made forests, mountains, prairies, rivers, and vast waters, filled them with animals and plants, then scattered the remains, in chaos, across the

Big Bend. The contorted landscape of today seems to confirm this theory, but the geologic genesis is even more astounding.

To the west lie Mesa de Anguila and Sierra Ponce, high fault-block plateaus of marine limestone, where the Rio Grande flows in a stone box. South, the river makes its big desert bend, carving through the same carbonate layers, which are tightly folded into Mariscal Mountain. East stands the Sierra del Carmen, with wave after wave of fault-fractured rock cut again by the winding river in Boquillas Canyon. North, past Persimmon Gap, the Santiago Range reaches toward the Davis and Guadalupe mountains, while at the center, like an island fortress, the high Chisos Mountains rise.

Compounded of Tertiary-age intrusions, lava flows, limestones, and clays, the Chisos Mountains are outliers of both the Rockies and the Sierra Madre. Spreading gravel fans, covered sparsely by sotol, cactus, lechuguilla, creosote bush, acacia, grasses, and mesquite, slope away from the peaks to the branched drainages of Tornillo Creek, Terlingua Creek, and the floodplains of the Rio Grande. Lichen-covered phantoms and desert spines intermingle here in obsolete time with maples, oak, fir, and pine.

One hot summer afternoon I walked with Ann, Tomijan Nabors, Alan Tillman, and Harold Crawford down to the Chisos Basin Window, where water plunges out to the desert below. Leaning back on streamside stone, we watched dry peaks draw clouds from the sky. Fallen rain danced besides us, reflecting cliffs marked by powers that raised old mountains above the plains, and I watched the mighty rocks wear down again, drawn toward the earth's dark center, grain by grain.

A river-cane flute, held to the Window's throat, played eerie melodies on the blowing air. The scent of nolina perfumed the breeze, and light pierced drops floating free. I read of prehistoric people who wove baskets, sandals, and clothing from desert fibers, and Ann made a tiny container of basketgrass, filled it with sweet blossoms, and placed it on the living plant as a simple greeting to weaving sisters long departed.

Two doves came to drink from the cascading water, rested, then flew out of spectral showers, circled high up, and disappeared. The cautious went back to camp as black clouds gathered, but I followed an obscure trail over the shoulder to the face beyond. Near sundown, rumbling clouds stormed the flank of Pulliam Ridge, a dark sky boiled down on Vernon Bailey Peak, and the wind abruptly dropped. Two hundred feet across the chasm, something shattered, again, then half a dozen times. Faint hissing grew into shrill screams that suddenly struck the rock behind me, and a sudden shower of hailstones exploded on the mountain. Thunder rolled, clouds broke, and shadows yawned east, swallowing the dying light. I walked slowly to camp, listening to the sounds of the night shift awakening and remembering the panther screams heard the previous evening.

During another trip to the park, on a grim November morning, I climbed with Harold Crawford and Mark Mason to Laguna Meadows as sharp winds and light sleet swept in. A Pacific cold front cleared the sky, and we reached the South Rim just in time to see the sun drop west of Sierra Ponce. Under a bright moon, temperatures plunged below freezing, alpine gales blew on for hours, and then sometime after midnight the winds quit.

Dawn broke clear, preceded by Venus, inner companion to the sun. In the dark hour of the wolf, tall grasses greeted me, fellow witnesses to the long preparation of our star to rise. A thin line spread into a dome that passed from pale gray through lavender and rose, then flamed up orange around the royal orb, awesome and unstoppable in its coming. As the day quickly warmed, a pair of red-tailed hawks glided by, surging on strong thermal currents. I wondered, What do they really feel? So, balanced on the rim, I held my breath, leaned into powerful, windy arms with my own arms wide outstretched, sprang lightly up, and briefly soared on the pleasure of flight.

Harold and Mark slowly unfolded after the cold, cramped night, and unable to photograph, we packed and split oranges for breakfast. Walking through waving meadows, I was elated, in spite of taking no pictures, having finally befriended my archfoe, the wind. Descending into Boot Canyon, we passed dazzling bigtooth maples quaking on autumn air, and west, below Emory Peak, the southernmost stand of aspens in the United States waved invisibly from the massive boulders of an old rock slide.

A cold wind flooded the canyon at sunset, and we bedded down early but awoke often to the sandy scurries of delicate rodent feet. In the silence before dawn I went up to first light. Agaves, decorated with fallen oak leaves, were luminous in the blue canyon glow. Spindly gray ball moss hung from smooth volcanic walls, and stoic cactus lay back on pine-needle beds. Overhead the rock caught fire, and gold reflections rippled on timeless waters.

Altogether unannounced, the midday pack train burst into my thoughts as a noisy horse ride arrived with children in sneakers, women in sandals, a man with a radio, and swarms of flies. One rider got off, dropped her reins, and let her mount stampede through camp. As the rest plodded past, we hurried to load and leave. At a notch between pinnacles, where the trail turns down, we rested and surveyed the unoccupied waste, determined to try it sometime, just for the peace and quiet.

The following February, out on the flats, Harold and I threaded our way through incredible lechuguilla gardens to an old stone corral that held only the dusty smell of oblivion. It was the most desolate place I have ever seen. There were not even insects or birds to fend off the omniscient emptiness.

We cooked on a loud stove that whistled and roared, and the silence deafened us when it quit. Harold built a small twig fire to placate the tangible loneliness, and glowing coals evoked thoughts unutterable elsewhere. We spoke of responsibility, family, and the need to get away to clearly see perspectives, but I tended to cloud the conversation with anxious interjections until Harold effectively called to my attention the fact that I could not really listen and think ahead at the same time.

The embers died, nothing stirred, and there was no sound we did not make ourselves. I lay under a thin net envelope, clothespinned to my bag, that I hoped would keep me safe from the scorpion stampedes. Only flat stones remained on the deflated mesa, but they were quite comfortable, and I soon forgot the marauders, snapping clothespins, and sagging net and drifted through remarkable cycles of sleep and alertness.

Harold slept heavily, having shouldered a surplus day pack without benefit of a padded hip belt or harness, but unable to lie quietly, I got up early and went off to explore. Something caught my attention, and I knelt beside a cactus where a golden spider was spinning her web.

Suspended, it seemed, at the end of a thread like a living cross-section through time was a tiny round earth that turned in the still light of dawn. At breakfast, Harold suggested I had just seen an ordinary spider catch an ordinary fly, but we both agreed that was no less extraordinary if true.

Davis Mountains

Surrounding Alpine with high volcanic ridges, the Davis Mountains hold the state's largest montane forests above arid western plains. Composed mostly of Tertiary-age lava flows, welded ash falls, and faulted granitic intrusions, some of which produced spectacular dissected domes, the rough regional topography resulted primarily from gradual erosion of softer sediments that once encompassed the resistant igneous masses. Differential weathering of old vertical joints has honed the rocks to sawlike edges and pinnacles, while arroyo downcutting due to sheep and goat overgrazing in the drought-plagued 1950's continues to undermine the native grasslands.

Very few prehistoric home sites have been identified or excavated in Jeff Davis County, which contains most of the Davis Mountains, but they include large and small caves, boulder shelters, and open lithic camps. Although vandals have obliterated the more accessible pictographs, some still show people, other animals, plants, and geometric designs. The most notable find in the area was a single cache of twelve hundred distinctive points that represent the first appearance of the bow and arrow in Trans-Pecos Texas. The tiny projectiles came to light along with a large blade and a few stone beads from a shallow pit on top of Mount Livermore.

In addition to transient vandalism, recent resort development threatens more than archaeological or biological inquiry. Mercury-vapor lights and smoke from brush fires already adversely affect astronomical research at McDonald Observatory on Mount Locke, and although it now has the greatest number of clear viewing nights of any similar facility in the United States, continued subdivision of surrounding ranchland could blind the great telescopes to further observation.

One August weekend I went with botanists Ron Hartman and Jackie Smith on a vegetational survey of the central Davis Mountains for Texas Conservation Foundation reports. Our primary objective was 8,382-foot-high Baldy Peak. We all left camp more or less together, but I lagged back, burdened by an old Graphic View camera and every gadget I could stuff into my pack. That giant workbeast of the photographic past was wonderful to use but heavy and hateful to carry up steep mountains.

The trail looked straightforward on two-dimensional maps, but I soon lost my way in the rocks, trees, and lesser features that never show up on printed pages. The sun disappeared early, and I began to call out in hesitation. But when I stopped, echoes faded, and I found myself alone in strange country for the very first time. I had no map or clear idea which way to go, other than up, or vaguely down in misplaced defeat.

So long as the climb was easy, I felt fine. It was while squeezing over ledges and pulling up tight fractures that I finally caved in. I pigged down some jerky and turned sick. Then, with my head splitting and stomach rolling, I stumbled into a hidden canyon where harebells and bluebells cascaded from the cliffs. Too dizzy to make any photographs, I stopped to watch a patch-nosed snake glide over dry pine and madrone leaves, and my knees checked out. I decided to camp and find the others in the morning. I chucked the pack and collapsed on brittle needles, but jumped up again as a palm-sized tarantula strolled out.

Despair shook me with imagined terrors. I might be attacked by pumas, bitten by snakes, stung by hornets, or starve. I could take sunstroke, die freezing on a summer night, go mad like the coyote in the well, or stumble off the mountainside. At the least, I would be alone, psychologically unprepared for only my own company. I sobbed until I laughed and then yelled out, "You jackass, you couldn't die when you wanted to; what makes you think it's going to happen now?" I shouted again and heard a startled reply. I had almost quit within sight of my friends.

They were glad to see me arrive with the stove. We cooked, but I could not eat. I just sat and breathed irregularly. The sky began to spin, I heaved several times, and by morning I was very weak. I forced a few pictures, then declined the final assault and instead lay in my bag, shivering in the warm winds.

About noon the others returned with excited reports of wild potatoes, nodding onions, and rare carrots. After a quick lunch that I also skipped, we hefted our packs, and I wobbled into an oak forest wind-bent to the rock. We stooped and dodged under a gray, leafy canopy until we emerged at resistant outcrops where we filled our canteens from mossy seeps and rested. I felt much better a thousand feet lower and ate a grapefruit that had been to the top and back.

As I lay in tall grasses framed by dark pines, with the sky vaulted to the zenith above me, I realized I had survived my own imagined nadir and had actually learned from it. To the external observer it was a casual overnight hike up a dry rock heap, complete with altitude sickness and fatigue, but I knew that someday every place would be my native home.

Sierra Diablo

Northwest of Van Horn, in the Sierra Diablo, cloudbursts and persistent winds have carved tortuous Victorio Canyon from an uplifted Permian ocean reef that rises steeply to more than six thousand feet above a closed salt basin on the east, then slopes gently westward into the Diablo Plateau. The striking relief of the arid limestone mountains is mostly the result of Mesozoic and Cenozoic block faulting subsequently modified by intense erosion and rapid deposition.

Isolated arroyos branch off the upper main draws of both Big and Little Victorio canyons and then narrow above five thousand feet into moist, fertile glens where stranded oak, fern, barberry, bigtooth maple, and madrone can be seen. The canyons and sierras lie geographically within the Chihuahuan biotic province, as do the Davis Mountains to the south, and animals of the lower elevations are typical of desert fauna. However, animals appear over the rim that are characteristic of the Guadalupe Mountains in the Navahoan biotic province to the north, indicating that the location and physical structures of the area have long made it a key stepping stone in the distribution of plants and animals between vast regions.

I went with a natural area survey team on a hot day in June toward J. V. McAdoo's pioneer homestead. We rode from the town of Sierra Blanca over the wide, brown Diablo Plateau through a cholla forest blooming head-high in magenta cactus flowers that opened at sunrise, spread at noon, then closed again at dusk. Roaring bees contended with relentless winds as I wandered up a slight rise to the edge of a bleak expanse, unprepared for what lay before me. The earth fell away as if stricken aeons ago by some huge hammer on the side of a gigantic anvil. The Sierra Diablo kept its secrets well, right to the end, then starkly revealed the truth. The gently tilted plateau contained hidden mountains just as the ancient seafloor involved latent plains waiting patiently over hundreds of millions of years to be realized.

An ignominious hollow near the rim marks the final battle site between Texas Rangers and the last of dead Chief Victorio's defeated Mescalero Apaches. It does not look particularly sacred despite the blood shed on that cold January day in 1881 when native American men, women, and children were shot to end their occupation of West Texas.

Archaeologists have found traces of cultivated corn, worked flints, and twisted fiber remnants in a bat cave on the outer escarpment, and inside a rattlesnake shelter they have located several partly defaced pictographs. Among the images still discernable are long-tailed elk, people hunting with spears, and a delightful red-ocher sheep with great curving horns that looks directly out at you from the prehistoric past.

J. V. McAdoo followed a hunch west to this sierra in the late long-grass heyday of the ranges, and with love for the land his family has endured, strong and solid. Jewell, his daughter, told me that as a child she watched the herds of bighorn sheep browse along steep ledges, adults and babies together, and when spooked, to her amazement they all plunged over the edges, skidding to impossible safety on front hooves, with their horns bowed down to noble stone.

Twenty-five years ago the last Texas bighorn sheep, native descendants of ancestors that survived post-Pleistocene hunters by nearly five thousand years, succumbed to bluetongue, a domestic sheep disease carried by gnats and introduced from the Old World with modern ranching. Well-adapted through thousands of years to wild demands, the bighorns had no immunity to the common microbes that plague our flocks. In 1939 three hundred Texas bighorns were counted in the Sierra Diablo. By 1956 the population had dropped to five individuals, and the following year they were extinct. How utterly alone the last bighorn must have been, a herd creature by nature, shaking on some howling rim, choking, without knowing why there were no others to share the lonely hour. Bereft of the swift dignity of death by fang and claw, it was left only solitary death by loathsome, invisible interlopers.

A Texas wildlife management area now occupies part of the Sierra Diablo, where bighorn sheep have been reintroduced from Arizona in an expensive attempt to repopulate barren mountains. The intent is to produce bragging trophies that favored sportsmen can hang in urban dens as proof of prowess never earned, while rightful predators like cougars, bobcats, coyotes, and wolves are wantonly destroyed. A broader, balanced view is needed, not for consumer sport and public recreation, but more urgently for protection, preservation, and sensitive propagation of the original inhabitants that flourished here and still give character to this rocky earth. They developed the environments we have prospered in, and they continue to sustain us today. If the remaining wild lands are lost, our oldest heritage will vanish forever, and with it integrity and perhaps our way to the future.

Salt Flats and Guadalupe Mountains

The harshest of all Despoblado environments are the salt flats that sink below the Sierra Diablo and Guadalupe Mountains. There, even creosote bush cannot take the halites, sulfates, and bare naked quartz of shifting playas. However, a few migrants like killdeers, shovelers, and avocets, more typical of seacoasts than of deserts, actually thrive. Tough, succulent halophytes have also adapted to the crystalline salt pans and casually withstand intense osmotic shocks from seasonal freshwater rains. Sporadically, miraculous brine shrimp hatch from eggs laid dormant in the crusty beds. They boil in shallow evanescent lakes, grow, cavort, lay eggs again in saline mud, and die as their world evaporates. Then like tiny bits of jade clustered in low places, millions of pale crustaceans bleach and drift in the sun—mute evidence of normal, local catastrophe.

As I stood on the salty sands, light filled everything with substance and heat. Cracks widened, dust devils gnawed at the playas, and silence was complete. Steel cans rusted, plastic crazed, and glass dissolved back into pastel rainbows. The discarded husk of an old photograph became a fashionable spider's house, and a weary dung beetle, cruising for food, rested temporarily in my shadow.

A mirage reflected the optical impostor of the far sierras, and as I walked forward, heat lakes receded where four weeks before hurricane rains rippled shin high. Thousands of acre-feet of water had evaporated at the amazing rate of about a quarter-inch a day, leaving only inverted ghosts to dance on hot horizons.

Thin clouds floated through Guadalupe Pass and then settled in slow motion to the basin below. Sandhill cranes circled over, seeking ancient bearings toward warmer ranges ahead of autumn snows, and for a moment their voices wove an eerie melody that stirred primal notions of early migrations from a time before calendars were made.

Partway up into the Guadalupes, creosote green katydid quonkers called bush-to-bush for late dates, but active desert sparrows interrupted by eating them. Old seed-grinding holes worn in the sandstone boulders told of human occupation by early hunters and gatherers who drifted through, but the true people of the Guadalupe Mountains were the wild Mescalero Apaches, whose dominion went virtually uncontested by early western explorers.

For centuries, Mescaleros camped by the life-giving springs and foraged among the peaks for game, adventure, and the agaves of their name. Even now, burned rock middens where they feasted on roasted hearts of the giant amaryllis are common throughout the Chihuahuan Desert. The mescal makers were warmly protective of their own people but pitilessly cruel to their enemies. Although raiding and war were integral to their predatory power and personal version of manifest destiny, they were not inarticulate savages; rather, they were likely the finest guerrilla warriors the world has ever known.

Consider what Cadete, a captured Mescalero Apache said: "You desire our children to learn only from books, and say that because you have done so, you are able to build all those big houses, and sail over the sea, and talk with each other at any distance, and do many wonderful things; now, let me tell you what we think. You begin when you are little to work hard, and work until you are men to begin fresh work. You say that you work hard in order to learn how to work well. After you get to be men, then you

say, the labor of life commences; then too, you build big houses, big ships, big towns, and everything in proportion. Then, after you have got them all, you die and leave them behind. Now, we call that slavery. You are slaves from the time you begin to walk until you die, but we are free as the air."

When easterners took interest in the West, things changed—for better or worse, depending on where you stand, or stood then. Captain Felix McKittrick brought his name to the most beautiful canyon in the Guadalupe Mountains in 1869, and then in 1876, just one hundred years after national independence, the Rader brothers built the first permanent ranch house at Ojo Frijoles. Spanish immigrants had come for centuries to the area for salt, but Anglos tried to enforce narrow ideas of personal possession on a universal resource, and the old Mexican inhabitants responded with the short Salt War of 1877. Fortunately other deposits were discovered, and the salt flats were abandoned to Indians, infrequent wagon trains, and, finally, survey teams searching for quick ways to the Pacific.

Bertha and Walter Glover moved to Pine Springs, near the abandoned Butterfield stage depot, in 1907. Walter is dead now, but Bertha and her grown daughter Mary still maintain the old family cafe and gas station. On my way through the pass, I stopped for a fill-up and cup of hot java. Bertha sat by the fire with a red-sweatered chihuahua when a traveler hurried in for beer and cigarettes and asked, "Does the wind always blow this way?"

"No," she answered, "sometimes it blows the other way." I saw her twinkle, and wink a sly grin, but the Dallas man missed it.

Mary operates a cloud seeder for a California weather company, and when storms show up on satellite pictures, somebody calls and says, "Turn it on and pull them in." During one early storm a cowboy came by to warm up and asked Mary if she was running the cloud machine. "Sure," she replied.

"Thanks a lot," he said, "I'm out there chasing strays through the cold, and you're growing snow."

North up the only road around is the Nickel Creek Cafe, recently reopened by the Burkhart family from Houston, who traded a salvage yard for clear air and open country where kids can grow up away from city crime. There is not a lot

19

of felony on the rural side of life, simply because it does not pay. Everybody pretty much knows everybody else, and although they are isolated, they are not insulated like apartment dwellers, jammed up six sides to the sky, so when need arises there is no question of aid.

I followed an oil exploration truck through Carlsbad to the Sitting Bull Falls turnoff and then went over in New Mexico to Dog Canyon, 125 miles from the main national park visitor center. I cut across El Paso Gap late in the afternoon as yellow snakeweed snickered in yards and around stock pens where the land was hardest bitten. Juniper and other brushy allies massed on the ridges and slid downslope into jagged agarita, tempting with ripe red berries, while pines and firs scattered up the canyons and western bigtooth maples crowded the rocky bottoms, limb to limb with eastern chinquapin oaks.

I carried my compact view camera up the recently flooded arroyo to a spring which was protected in a green steel box shaped like a tank turret. It somehow seemed odd that a spring which existed thousands of years without armor now needs buffering from the direct body contact of people and the cobblestone cannonades of high-water erosion.

Dog Springs contrasted starkly with another on the outer escarpment where water flows to the surface, swirls in fern-lined pools, and then plunges toward the Pecos Valley only to disappear in the sand. There, the essence of life appears, offers itself incidentally to all creatures, and then quietly returns to the earth. Tears fell in the stream, and I paid close attention, intensely aware that I was near the very heart of things, blessed to let the woman of me weep and show the man tenderness to temper strength.

I trudged up Lost Peak on the bright gashes of newly bulldozed trails that zigzagged across the bare backs of the ranges. Scars forever, in human terms, those wide paths will also influence erosion and restructure wild animal migration for as long as the mountains stand. Towering on the shoulders of humanity, a solitary person could remake the face of this earth by the casual touch of a button. Any weekend, with a little power boost, the rest of us can rent machines to push the planet around just about any way we want to, and frontier law backs us up with private ownership rights, but possession in western terms is absurd.

If anything, land owns the owners, especially if they try to force produce or animal profits from it. Contemporary agrarian life still demands the harsh husbanding kind of love that first broke the plains to collectively feed our hungry mouths. But old Teutonic ways that tried to conquer the world with a humble blade let much more food be grown in one season than could be eaten, and now ironically an explosion of humans swells in the wake of modern tractors that roll down dusty rows just ahead of starvation.

Later, from Wilderness Camp Ridge north of the Texas state line, I looked across eroded limestone fins past dry plains and the Delaware basin to a light horizon where a hundred miles away the Davis Mountains formed an irregular dark mass. White-throated swifts flashed by on arrowed wings like green obsidian, and agitated ants, out for drinks after drought-busting rains, criss-crossed the ground.

Sundown came hazy, cold and uneasy, with a change promised from the east. The rocky ledge I camped on in the national forest was covered with charcoal pits thick as moon craters, so I conjured a bright companion in still air. Fire is time warped as energy escapes and solar heat, laid slowly by for years, burns holes in the cosmic cloak. Leaping back through history to heartwood, it turns darkness into day.

Blinded, I held my hand to the blaze and squinted west, where El Paso glowed, a pale offense in the black sky. Dying coals scintillated at my feet, car lights crept through empty valleys half a mile below, meteors flared overhead, glancing off our all-sustaining atmospheric membrane, and like a river of stars, the Milky Way ran pole to pole. It is never truly dark, I thought, wherever there are living beings. Fog rolled slowly in with a lost-continent feeling and froze the ridges into silent islands of unseen relict creatures.

Bound for maples next day, I happened by on the McKittrick Canyon trail as a young geologist lectured to a field class slumped on the rocky hillside. I slowed my pace as he shouted, arms waving, "Although the Guadalupe Mountains have long been called the world's largest reef, so far no classic structure can be found." The Texas champ may not really be a reef, maybe more of a gigantic calcareous mud bank, locally abundant in sponges, algal bioherms, and marine associates typical of reefs, but rich in overall entropy.

After three hundred million years, the mountains were scarcely moved, and it only slightly altered the big picture of the Permian–El Capitan Complex that built out, intermittently, over its own broken talus in response to fluctuations of a transgressive-regressive ocean basin that eventually dropped two thousand feet in places. Submarine canyons carried turbidity flows along lines colinear with current transverse valleys where forests now grow, and for millions of years waves broke on the crest of the escarpment. Then the region tilted and uplifted, and sediments accumulated from northern mountains and buried all but the tops of Texas' tallest peaks.

Mesozoic seas returned to lay down limestones that mostly washed away as the Trans-Pecos region rose at the close of the Cretaceous period. Tertiary uplifts then hastened erosion and complicated Permian structures with massive faults and fractures that eventually dissolved into immense caverns, while from the south, volcanos spread fine ash over the whole Despoblado. Again in the Pliocene epoch, the Guadalupes were temporarily buried under bolson fill until the young Pecos River began to remove sediment in the Pleistocene and exhumed the silent mountains of today.

I surprised an ouzel dipping for crustaceans in a flood-sculptured basin and saw the silver-feathered ghost walk, bubble-covered, on the bottom where rainbow trout darted from sunlight to shade. Farther on, startled mule deer clattered up a rocky slope to cover in a skeleton forest of dying pine. The canyon was constricted above Turtle Rock and hung with lush reeds, ferns, orchids, cardinal flowers, and frost-browned columbine. Upstream from the narrows it is too fragile to ever enter safely, and there on the weathered cliff, appealing to the intellect, is a small battered sign:

STAY OUT

FRAGILE BIOLOGICAL AREA

DO NOT GO BEYOND THIS POINT

Human footprints led over the gravel beyond the sign, into the heart of the sanctuary. My rage flared uselessly, but I stayed for a long time smoothing the ground so others could discover an unmarked place as though for the very first time. Light reddened, the day ended, and I realized it was too late to climb out to my assigned camp without breaking my neck on the trail. I had to stay the night in paradise but leave no trace behind.

As night fell on the steep walls, I felt as if something big knew about my unscheduled presence. I ate cold vegetables for dinner, nothing I thought a carnivore would like, and then at seven o'clock, with no fires permitted, rolled into my sack and stretched out. Cold air poured in, stirred by gusty winds, mares' tails raced over the rim, and I tossed for hours before finally sliding into unconsciousness.

Unannounced in the unreal hours, the moon struck the cliffs, colorless, bright as day. Half asleep, I went on drifting and then, as though falling, suddenly started awake, aware that I was not alone. I heard feet pad softly on bare stone and sticks crack in a maple thicket. Waiting, I listened, but silence caught my ears. My eyes searched among the shadows, and I recognized a familiar shape, elusive, hauntingly beautiful, terrifyingly strange. A hollow screamed inside my heart, and the old hushed longing crept close to the edge of night. Take me, life, I thought. Do as you will, but use me some way with love. Do not let me go useless, back into the earth. Fill me first with light. I want to see before darkness eases pain.

Trapped, like bait in the twilight, I could not move, although I saw what appeared to be a huge cat, crouching nervously. It can't be real, I told myself, only imagined out of fear, but I lay so still my back ached, and I brooded on tales of a fresh-killed doe found partly covered on the same path I should have taken before dark. I was easy prey, but the cougar did not want me. I believe it was actually just curious to know more about a creature crazy enough to sleep on a stream bed in a panther's backyard. Before sunrise, outlasted, I nodded off with adrenaline fatigue, and when I finally awoke, the empty maple grove was only full of light.

El Paso and Hueco Mountains

Bright star to most people in the Despoblado, the bilingual metropolis of El Paso–Juárez, colonial mother to over a million thirsty souls, sits astride the shrunken Rio Grande at the famous northern pass between Monte Cristo Rey and Sierra de la Otra Banda. There, ninety percent of the region's human inhabitants crowd into two percent of its space. Founded in 1659 as a small Spanish mission, it is now a modern anomaly strangely out of place.

As I eased south from New Mexico one autumn along the edge of the El Paso military-industrial maze, a dark van swerved past me and abruptly pulled over. A huge man and woman, dressed in camouflage clothes, got out, took a few steps to the shoulder, and fired semiautomatic rifles into the dunes I had hoped to photograph. I went instead to crowded Scenic Drive Overlook for an unexpected view of moonrise over McDonald's and passionate teenagers making out, creating their own urban privacy by getting high on Friday night.

Cold, round, and deathly beautiful, the waxing moon lifted slowly above the eastern horizon, serene beyond the noise and rush, just as it may in the not-too-distant future rise over the empty remains of the twin sun cities, where there is not enough water to quench the ever-growing thirst of so many active people. Folks in big towns live in such an artificial world, remote from the one that maintains us, that it taxes reason to believe the two coexist in time and space. They scarcely touch, in fact, except along the frayed edges, where streets dead end and brush thrives and wild things go about unseen because only the Starmaker watches.

Strung out on powerlines across the bolson floor, sparking colors rippled in the biting wind. Like a phosphorescent reef or great jellyfish, the city seemed to pulse in a restless sea, and jets with brilliant lights stabbed out of the night like UFOs, every bit as impressive as any second coming could be. Cowboy jet jockeys are fundamental successors to old horse soldiers up from Mexico and out from the East. Their insane game is still the same; only the weapons have changed, to better protect the innocent. Atoms and deserts can both be conceived of as desolate wastes of enormous emptiness, yet neither is sterile. They are fertile voids from which life naturally evolves and into which it may gracefully dissolve unless swords or plowshares prematurely bury us all.

From my camp in the Hueco Mountains I watched fireballs rise throughout the night over White Sands Missile Range. One, two, three at a time they wavered down, then flashed behind the Organ Mountains. Early next morning, tired and agitated, I hiked out of sight to a hidden valley, a little *potrero* where a netleaf hackberry offered shade, surrounded by oaks, sotol, ocotillo, cloakfern, yucca, cholla, and mesquite. White-throated wood rats gathered ripe grasses around fat collared lizards that lay sunning on crystalline rocks.

Geologically, the Hueco Mountains are made of Pennsylvanian-, Permian-, and Cretaceous-age carbonates deposited between 320 million and 135 million years ago. They were uplifted by Laramide compression folding less than 100 million years back, and then about 34 million years before the present, Tertiary-age batholiths, dikes, and sills intruded. Basin-and-range block faulting, 20 million years ago, began to expose the fine-grained domes, and recent erosion reveals intimate contacts between the igneous and the host rock.

Unable to shake the frenzied city, I explored the miniature ranges and closed weathered basins, or *huecos*, and high up I stumbled onto several late-drying pools that teemed with chitinous aquatic life. Some creatures looked like newly sprouted bean seeds, green with frilly legs and waving antennae, while others were long and minnow-shaped, with orange forked tails and thousands of cilia that undulated rhythmically along their ventral sides. Most remarkable of all were the small armored tadpole shrimp, in exoskeletons resembling hybrids of horseshoe crabs and trilobites, that kicked and bit as they twisted, turned, and mated, trying to evade the inevitable sun. They fornicated their own last rites, then dined like cannibal lovers on family and friends in an orgy of life before the end and cast out eggs to colonize the future. Left over, like Noah's metaphorical children, from a time when dying seas flooded this whole land, they may have adapted to declining tides by selectively learning to live intermittent lives in part-time pools, repeating in a few short days a cycle millions of years old, but they cannot long survive, artificially revived. They must wait instead for the timely gift of rain in shallow worlds just six feet on a side.

Something human that has not changed, at least in thousands of years, is the basic desire to achieve immortality. Vivid pictographs decorate certain boulders with palm prints, cosmic spirals, suns, lightning bolts, serpents, and a man in black with a three-cornered hat. More recently, vandals with spray cans and chisels have inscribed their names, and even Isleta pueblo kids have scrawled on the ancient images in desperation, unaware that we really leave the greatest mark in all we leave untouched. From messages left by ancient artists, however, archaeologists have determined that the rounded Hueco hills supported a unique farming community tied harmoniously to the watered land. Self-sufficiency afforded primitive occupants ample time for an art uniquely varied in wealth of imagery. When freed from base survival, they turned to beauty, explored the realm of symbols that surfaced from their humanity, and shared with us the significance of their lives. Look, they said, we were here. We had hands and eyes, and the land was beautiful, and we were the land and beautiful too. Now they are gone, and the land is beautiful, as always, but who will ever see or feel what they knew?

Rio Grande

In the dry valley southeast of El Paso several small irrigated farming settlements have grown, suckling on the Rio Grande floodplains, but agriculture empties the Great River completely for hundreds of miles below Fort Quitman—all the way, in fact, to La Junta de los Ríos at Presidio, where the older Río Conchos enters from Mexico. A few springs touch the surface between with life-giving waters, but they are rare, isolated oases.

In May one year I paid a visit with my psychic and adventurous friend Gath Anna Parmenas to famous Indian Hot Springs, once owned by millionaire health addict H. L. Hunt. A whitewashed bathhouse stands on the sparkling flats next to low mineral vats formed by salty ojos that used to spill unimpeded from the earth. I poked my nose through the pig-wire fence and peered into a black, bubbling hole which the puffy caretaker said went straight down over a mile.

The blue tiled bathhouse was antiseptically efficient, and the astringent waters felt mighty medicinal, but the watchman's squinty vigilance inhibited exploitation of the facilities. Soaking, however, it was easy to imagine what relief the rude springs must have brought to Apaches for whom they are named. Individual ojo openings were originally assigned to levels of social hierarchy according to decreasing surface temperature. Chief, Beauty, and Squaw are dandy, but contrary Stump, at 120 degrees Fahrenheit, flows the hottest in Texas.

Feeling like pickled herring, we left before sundown and camped on high desert between the Eagle and Quitman mountains where angular ridges of fractured Cretaceous limestone abutted Tertiary igneous rocks. Not much remains there of the burned wagon trains or hostile Apaches that made Quitman Pass the most dreaded part of travel from San Antonio to El Paso in the latter half of the nineteenth century. Migrating settlers related frightening stories of Indian attacks, intense loneliness, and ominous sounds in the dark Canyon of Sorrows.

Soldiers were assigned to protect people streaming west to California but found that their ignorance of the varied landscapes, and eastern horses, hampered a gallant style of wide-open combat. To counter the guerrilla genius of the native insurgents, a brilliant quartermaster decision was made to try camels. Lieutenant Echols in 1860 led an experimental cavalry caravan of camels, horses, and mules to see which performed best. The expedition got lost, the equines nearly died, the men did a little better, but the camels thrived, carrying water for everyone else. They developed a taste for creosote bush, ignored rattlesnake bites, and although deprived of water themselves, enabled the rest to survive.

Despite their cantankerous natures, they were actually right at home, since camels evolved hereabouts, fifty million years ago, and were probably glad to get back. In the confusion of the Civil War, Washington failed to appreciate their appropriateness for desert use, not to mention the psychological effects they must have had on astonished Indians. After the Camel Corps disbanded, the animals were scattered, and some escaped and founded short-lived dynasties. Eventually most died at the muzzles of guns, although one was seen in 1910 in a San Antonio sideshow, and another was captured far to the west, in the Sonoran Desert, in 1917.

In the silent spring, Gath and I circled the Rio Grande rimrock country through Van Horn and Lobo to Marfa and then headed south toward Pinto Canyon between Chinati Peak and the Sierra Vieja. Pavement soon ended in gravel, and startled mule deer gracefully bounded into arroyos as we rumbled past. Then the rolling, grassy plains abruptly ended. Down the rim, toward the river, brush grew thicker, thornier, and more defensive. Hungry red-tailed hawks watched for rodents from daggered yuccas and flowering lechuguilla, and scrawny cows turned to stare, blankly chewing cholla. Thousands of strawberry pitaya cactuses bloomed along the riverbanks, their flowers full of beetles, bees, wasps, and flies that staggered out intoxicated on golden pollen.

After a picture break we followed a grocery-laden pickup truck over the dusty road to the village of Candelaria at the very end of nowhere. Frances Howard and Marion Walker, remarkable sisters, have operated the eighty-year-old Kilpatrick family store there since 1948. Stacks of straw hats tower to a tin roof over pots, pans, steel-canned foods, notions, lotions, linens, hardware, *refrescas*, *helados*, and candy colorful enough to please any child.

If you are sincere at heart and want to meet people in new places, first make friends with children. If they accept you, so will everyone else. Ask Jonnie Chambers, who runs sixty-four thousand acres of family ranch with her husband Boyd in addition to educating young Candelarians in a one-room, all-grades schoolhouse.

No doubt, it takes strong men to live along the Rio Grande, but the women here are uncommonly resourceful. Mrs. Chambers acknowledges, "The desert is not for everyone. Some grow weary of it quickly, but for others, it becomes the only place to find peace. If you are meant to live here, once you drink the river, it always calls you back. But if you don't love it, you can't stay."

As if to prove a point, upriver where the Sierra Vieja crowds down on the Rio Grande, in the driest part of the Despoblado, one stormy night the ghostly river got out of its restless bed and took the road away. It has been that way since hasty engineers attempted to channel irregular banks, and now normal runoff upstream means flash floods below.

Hidden on private, well-protected land in the nearby rimrock country, water has patiently carved a natural cathedral from faulted Tertiary volcanic stone thousands of feet thick. Where a small perennial creek cascades more than one hundred feet over resistant rhyolite, calcium carbonate has formed a fragile stone cape, for which Capote Canyon is named. For countless generations, as slightly mineralized water plunged into desert air and evaporated, algae interacted photosynthetically to precipitate travertine, and the tall formation crystallized, layer by thin layer.

The creek emerges from small, marshy springs in the cienega above the falls, and although a few deep thermal seeps surface in the lower canyon, most of the flow comes from infrequent rainfall concentrated in Quaternary sediments above the impermeable volcanic rock. In the 1960's, after long drought and overgrazing, earth dams in the basin failed under flash floods, dumping tons of loose gravel down the cape. A deep pool at the bottom filled with sediment, and the *capote* itself began to crumble away.

Capote Canyon is still a unique riparian habitat, isolated in the Chihuahuan Desert, where the delicate mystery of water transforms arid scrubland into a wild, uplifting sanctuary. Although surrounded by extremely xeric flora, the slender stream supports lush stands of seep-willows, tules, cardinal flowers, foxtails, fewhead goldenrods, and sharp-edged sawgrass. Cliff frogs live high up in moist recesses, while spadefoot toads and barred tiger salamanders stay closer to the bottom. Turtles, lizards, and snakes abound, and eagles used to soar over, looking for rodents and droves of sheep, according to ranchers. That was before hired killers with airplanes shotgunned the feathered predators from the sky.

I first came to Capote Canyon late one evening in need of reloading exposed film holders, but a spritely red rain spattered mud and made changing outdoors impossible. Some rowdy visitors were whooping it up in the ruined adobe at the canyon mouth, and when I asked if I could come inside to switch film, they agreed. While I worked, we talked about the countryside. I confided the whereabouts of another lovely place, but the tedium of my task soon bored my hosts, and they resumed their own conversations. Paying them close attention was my own downfall, although I did not know until two weeks later, from double exposures, how badly distracted I really had been. It was not tall tales that brought me grief; rather, it was evidence of their hard day's rape.

They were inexperienced botanists and camping cohorts from a little central Texas college, and they were out on ill-directed attempts to collect voucher specimens for the school herbarium and incidental immortality by getting their names enshrined as well. Quietly I sat trapped in my bag of deceptions and watched horrified as they pulled rare creatures from sacks and forced them into blotter stacks for the night.

When huge bruised armfuls of endemic columbine came out of one pack, I protested, "Why so much?"

"To be sure of representative samples," the leader replied, but he lied. I saw it in his shifty eyes and furtive manner. The raw blind greed of collectors possessed them all.

Alone next morning I followed fresh cat tracks to the pour-off through rustling cottonwoods and willows that smelled of hot bees and sweet flowers. Water brought grace to hard land, smoothing bars and bedrock, slowly taking the edge off, but new scars marked the places where helpless lives had been taken from mist below the falls.

Deadly desert Baileya showed bitter gold at the base of the Chinati caldera, where I sampled the noisy mineral waters of Ruidosa Hot Springs, among the purest and most *caliente* in the region. The old stone cabins were managed by the Reverend and Mrs. Morehead, earnest people who treasured their freedom and rural right "not to do anything one certain way." The reverend liked to rise after midnight and take his worldly news from radio waves that only descend on the Despoblado in the dark hours when the ionosphere is quiet. Daylight excites the ethers too much to let electric messages bend around the mountains, so most of Trans-Pecos Texas lies in an instant-media shadow, mercifully screened from the world outside.

Southwest of Presidio, at Redford, whose real name is El Polvo ("the dust"), I once stopped at Enrique Madrid's store with crusty old Bill Porterfield, a journalist friend from Dallas. A quarter of the room was filled by used books, neatly stacked in plastic milk crates, and Bill was drawn past material merchandise to a world of ideas, where he browsed like a goat over the range of titles, then selected *The Portrait of a Lady* by Henry James. He meandered up to the counter and said, "I'll buy these," depositing the book, a knife, and a bag of tostados.

"You can have the knife and chips," Señor Madrid answered, "but you can't keep the book, although you can check it out if you want to, from our Biblioteca del Polvo."

Intrigued, Bill explained that we were just passing through. Enrique assured us that it did not matter, because the novel could be mailed back. He called his wife Lucía, who keeps the library, and showed us into their gracious home behind the store. It was lined from ceiling to floor with books, rocks, and artifacts. Upon seeing our surprise, Lucía smiled and said, "We have a passion for the history of this place."

The señora's family, the Redes, settled in El Polvo after her great-grandfather escaped twenty years of Apache captivity, and she told me, "I too was born by the Río Bravo and grew up here. I went to school here, and then became a teacher. That is how I learned the value of shared knowledge."

While Bill listened to family history, Enrique Junior showed me some of the fossils he has identified and a wooden Tarahumara traveling ball that an Indian kicked across the desert from Mexico to trade for canned tea and crackers. Then Enrique Junior's wife Ruby guided me through the garden, where she propagates native species and observes their adaptive ways. They have wisely laid by an invaluable treasure for the children of their valley against the unformed needs of tomorrow in an age when momentary pleasure is of principal concern.

Colorado Canyon

A little down from El Polvo the broad Rio Grande enters Colorado Canyon, the first major river obstruction of the Texas Big Bend, as it slices through the red-layered flanks of the extinct Bofecillos Volcano. Looking back, we can envision limestone foundations for the unborn Rio Grande deposited as fossiliferous ooze, clay, and small amounts of sand on the floor of a warm, shallow sea that sank at about the rate of accumulation in the immense late Mesozoic Mexican Geosyncline. For sixty million years or more, Cretaceous sediments gathered up to three miles thick. Then about one hundred million years ago, the Laramide Orogeny began to lift the stratified ocean bed above sea level, and erosion replaced deposition.

Land along the continental divide gradually buckled into the sky, deflected prevailing westerly winds, precipitated moisture, and gave rise, fifty to thirty million years ago in the Paleocene, Eocene, and Oligocene epochs, to a complex drainage system of significant size that carried sediments down from the young sierras to the sinking Rio Grande Embayment in the Gulf of Mexico. Shortly after Laramide uplift exposed Mesozoic limestones to erosion, Tertiary magmas intruded along bedding planes in the sedimentary strata and locally folded old Paleozoic formations, as well as younger Cretaceous seafloor, into domes and monoclines.

Early volcanos began to erupt nearby, and then suddenly, from vents in the Chinati caldera, a single or closely spaced series of inconceivably violent eruptions spread Mitchell Mesa ignimbrite over more than three thousand square miles. As hot magma rose out of incredible confining pressures deep in the crust, a point of phase change was reached, and dissolved water exploded into superheated steam that atomized the molten rock. Upon ejection from the earth, glowing ash particles outgassed and moved downslope in suspension at more than one hundred miles an hour. When steam and gasses finally cooled out of the surging cloud, hot ash fell and fused to the ground as monolithic ignimbrite or welded tuff. Thus, hundreds or even thousands of feet of juvenile crust were created in an awesome seething holocaust, perhaps in the time of an afternoon picnic.

The infant Bofecillos Volcano erupted the Fresno Formation, and then, from searing vents in Mexico, the Santana welded tuff was violently emplaced, also in the wink of a geologic eye. Finally, Bofecillos eruptions scattered intricately interfingered associations of ash and lava, concluding with the upper Rawls Formation.

The ancient rivers were interrupted as Middle Cenozoic volcanism exhausted gassy magmas. Trans-Pecos Texas began to tilt, fault, and settle, along with the rest of the Old West, and by Miocene time, basin-and-range tectonics completely broke the Laramide streams into closed bolsons fed by captive flows. For millions of years intermittent playa lakes slowly rose on gritty detritus that tumbled to their shallow bottoms, and eventually they built up thousands of feet to overflow and escape at the lowest divides. Other lakes filled and spilled, again into adjacent basins, cut more divides, excavated peaks, entrenched canyons, and, with planetary patience, re-created a through-flowing path from the mountains to the sea.

Dwight E. ("Big") Deal, a geologist and river friend who knows a lot first-hand about Despoblado rock, wrote, "It is likely that the Río Conchos, fed by rainfall in the mountains southwest of Chihuahua, reached the Presidio area before the Rio Grande, which was fed by snow-melt to the north in the southern Rocky Mountains. The ancestral drainage of the Río Conchos (or Rio Grande) then probably proceeded to fill the Presidio Bolson with a lake which overflowed in turn across the divide southeast of Presidio into a lower basin downstream, somewhere in the vicinity of what is now Big Bend Park. Similarly, the river proceeded to spill generally eastward until it finally overflowed into the headwaters of some tributary of the previously mentioned ancestral Rio Pecos–Río Conchos that drained into the Gulf of Mexico. It is quite likely that this integration occurred somewhere near what are now the lower canyons of the Rio Grande."

The overall appearance of the Big Bend gorges has changed very little since a U.S. Geological Survey team first successfully navigated them in 1899. With three wooden boats and five brave men, Robert T. Hill set out in October from Presidio, defying rumors of bandits and impassable chasms where the river was swallowed in caves. Many weeks later, by Langtry, hungry and benumbed, yet knowing what no other humans knew about the inner configuration of the river, they found the landmark of their journey's end: "a huge pile of sticks skillfully intertwined into what is perhaps the largest bird's nest in America" at Eagle Nest Canyon near Judge Roy Bean's Jersey Lilly Saloon.

I once captained an unusual paddleboat crew through Colorado Canyon for Uncle Steve Harris and Michael Davidson, pioneer cofounders of Far Flung Adventures of Terlingua ghost town. With able-bodied boatm'am par excellence Nancy Jane Reid, we guided school kids exploding out of Austin on a first class trip. Left turn, right turn, back, forward, stop. They caught on quickly to the basic boating commands. Bright, spirited, eager explorers, they were still quite innocent, although not always benevolent, and undeniably eager water fighters. Blades shook loose in the heat of one battle, and a young woman was so drenched she nearly became hypothermic. I covered her with a spare life jacket and my wind shell, and she knelt on the floor of the raft. Briefly she shivered in a trancelike sleep, then revived from some deep source and rejoined the continuing sport.

Bubbling exuberantly through the old volcano, they fired a thousand questions at me as I tried to describe the natural canyon refuge and downstream sanctuary of Big Bend Park. My crew clearly understood that their future resources lay isolated in public lands, set tenuously aside for coming demands by farsighted legislators, in the form of wilderness areas. Young folks today are not all unaware. They see the way the world cookie crumbles in their parents' hands and know that when they finally are admitted to adulthood, they might not have much to count on. One discouraged young man asked, "What can we do about things anyway? It will all be blown up before we have a chance." I said that sounded like too much TV and told him to love the world no matter what and get to know it well, like a pal, or his own backyard. If it is too late, then worrying won't help, but if it's not, giving up could hurt.

Santa Elena Canyon

I have guided campers along the length of the Rio Grande, from Colorado to the Gulf of Mexico, but the single worst human impact I ever witnessed was at the upriver entrance to Santa Elena Canyon one Easter weekend when hundreds of people squirmed elbow to eyeball on a fire-blackened sandbar about the size of a dance floor. In two spring days a pristine beach became a "stinking desert," to quote Ken Sabe Smith, and the spoils went to ants, flies, rats, and other scavengers hooked on human dole. Wild things become dangerously bold from repeated contact, and with nowhere else to go, things always come to push and shove.

Use brings abuse, and there is no way the river can remain free and clean, maintained as an uncontrolled recreational resource. Regulations are distasteful, especially to people seeking temporary freedom from urban restrictions; however, the very life of the river, and all it sustains, hangs on the balance. It is an intimate privilege to enter the inner flow of a wild gorge, and the consequence of being rude is everlasting. The river is not an anonymous victim to rape in idle sport. It is a lovely mother, radiant with unborn life, to be loved and protected. But make no mistake, for like most wild women, rivers are by no means weak or defenseless.

I was cutting up fruit salad by the bank one day on a Far Flung trip through Santa Elena Canyon when a rented plastic fleet of orange canoes happened by with obnoxious crews who popped tops, swilled beer, and sank the empties in the river. "Hey," I said, "that's not legal or considerate. Park regulations require that you carry out all trash."

"You can if you want to, buster, but we don't have room," a red face grunted.

"The river will get you," I shouted back, caught up in personal anger. Bottled bravery is the most popular way first-timers ease the stress of urban withdrawal and suppress Big Burger attacks, but alcohol can provoke serious misunderstandings between otherwise agreeable folks by blocking coherent communication.

In fact, that evening at the campfire I had a senseless argument with a tipsy man who loudly belched his desires for the genocide of wasps because one landed harmlessly on his sweaty shirt.

"Kill 'em all," he slurred. "We's can do without those buzzing things that bite."

Politely, I said bees and wasps don't usually bite, they sting, and that he would have to die to get his wish, along with everything else that depends on insect pollination. Suddenly we were toe to toe, and it looked like a fight until Catfish Callaway, head boatman and ace theater director, defused the scene and sat us both down to eat in uneasy silence.

Early the next morning, after a big coffee breakfast, my sober crew eased slowly through the upper Rock Slide and paid close attention as we pulled out safely in the middle to look at the trickiest obstacle on the whole lower river. Thousands of years ago huge blocks of rock split off the sixteen-hundred-foot-high sheer walls and collapsed into the narrow canyon throat, forming an immense sieve, or rock garden, that all but stops the whole river's flow. In normal low water there is only one safe shot between polished limestone boulders that loom above the rubber rafts, but it is always best to scout and avoid the unexpected. To our surprise, upside down at the bottom was an abandoned orange canoe, wagging forlornly, pinned to a razor fin that divided the river in two.

As we maneuvered through Fat Eddie's whirlpool casino toward the turbulent payoff slot, I delivered my "How to Keep Your Noble Hides" lecture. Don't be fooled, I warned, you are ultimately at the mercy of the river and can do nothing without her consent. Stay on the currents that go where we want to be, and avoid all the rest, or she will crush us without even knowing. I saw the others tighten for a moment and watched their knuckles whiten, but they pulled together for a safe, clean run.

On another trip during muddy floods, I eased into the churning currents to retrieve a young paddler who got washed overboard. I heaved him back and then, with the help of another lad, pulled myself up just in time to avoid the dread pouroff. Unfortunately, less than a week later at the same rapid, a stubborn, inexperienced fisherman in a flat-bottomed johnboat refused to take advice and drowned himself.

My fondest recollections, though, are of water and light and pure, naked rock, burning in the shadows of stars, moist tamarisk fragrant on warm winds, ripples in sandy coves, and the sigh and moan of irresistible forces twisting and rolling around huge boulders, dark oceans opened, vaulted seabeds cleaved, and sky drifting pale beyond. Whatever we bring, the river returns, and always in full measure.

Mariscal Canyon

Archaeologists, biologists, and geologists are the only people who travel slower and stop more often than I, so I thoroughly enjoy their company in the field. Unfortunately, on one interdisciplinary sweep from Lajitas to Boquillas, the survey went exceedingly slow. It took us three days to get through Santa Elena Canyon in canoes, and some of the party became discouraged by a long portage over the Rock Slide.

A sudden change of plans was announced, and I was told our expedition would end early at Tally, upstream of Mariscal Mountain, instead of at Rio Grande Village. A message was sent by walkie-talkie for the overland contingent to rendezvous at the newly appointed terminus. "No way," I yelled, "I signed on for a two-canyon run," and everyone sensed my displeasure.

I soon traded anger for curiosity, though, when we stopped at a hot silt terrace to scan for signs of human occupation. Evidence is everywhere that once offered useful resources, but major finds are few and far between. However, just about noon on the last day, the archaeologists found what they were looking for. At a plain site near an old low-water crossing we discovered tepee rings of reddish volcanic stone. Some A.D. 500 points came to light, and I saw a small tip dating to about 500 B.C., but the real

treasure nearly went unnoticed. Weathered, half-buried, a perfect clay vessel lay drifted full of sand. It was roughly squash-shaped and crudely fired, yet an elegant statement clearly understood by those who made it and ourselves, thousands of years behind. It felt warm, as if its maker had just handed it to us, new across the centuries, function intact, form quite pleasing, earthly origin powerful beyond words.

The archaeologists' hearts were pounding, and Bob Mallouf had to sit for a smoke. Barbara Baskin said the closest previous find of that kind was upriver at Redford. Virginia Wolfkule danced over the desert like an excited elf, searching for more, and smiling widely, Jimmy Jalapeeno took pictures of it all. In a single act of discovery, human knowledge leaped a hundred miles beyond the barrier of Santa Elena Canyon, thought until that moment to be the southernmost boundary of Puebloan river culture.

I wandered back to the canoes with buoyant illustrator Hal Story, noted botanist Marshall Johnston, and cunning linguist Anders Saustrup. We walked through dense mesquite thickets, seeing wetback cans and bottles in a new light. Refuse, now revered as art, reveals to us what was humbly significant and intimate to ancestral daily life and shows that reality is never in objects, only in their use. The truth of an idea lies in the space it beautifully fills, for life is the only real art, and all else is mere artifact.

It is impressive to see how much a trained observer can read in fragments of extinct cultures. Every point and chip tell something, not just grossly that people were here, but also from numbers and distribution, the intensity and purpose of use. Nothing is trivial in reconstruction, so after making sketches and photographs we replaced everything except for the fragile pot, which was wrapped and carefully removed to museum safety. Federal antiquities codes make it illegal and expensive for unauthorized persons to remove, disturb, or deface artifacts in this country, and Mexico has stiffer penalties and tougher jails, but laws are kept or broken according to the larceny of individual hearts.

Amateur collectors ignorantly tear holes in the human record, misguided by repeated desires to reach out and touch the very ones they forever alienate. Finders keepers does not work, because it means everybody loses in the end. There is no such thing as private archaeological property.

Paradoxically, the past belongs to all of us, to none of us, and to no one at all.

Desert heat cranked up late in the day and wispy clouds blew toward us from the west, but the overland contingent arrived at Tally, as rescheduled, with fresh food and cold brews. While the others untied, I swilled a few too many in the mad-dog sun and shed my clothes and inhibitions together. A quiet blush of anger recurred at being cheated out of Mariscal Canyon. I mumbled something about being at someone else's mercy, then realized the potential of the moment. Standing nearly naked, in a hat and sneakers at the stern of my borrowed boat, I announced my intention to continue alone. It was all so logical, almost inevitable. My car was still at the lower end, and I had food, film, and desire enough to complete our truncated, though highly successful, expedition.

At first no one took me seriously, but when I went around borrowing extra vittles, spare water bottles, and a backup paddle, folks saw I meant business. Persuasion and threats failed to sway me, so they took back all the articles of value they had loaned and left me with their own borrowed dregs. I admit it did not bolster my self-confidence much, but I was committed. The Reverend Dr. Johnston said I probably should be, for my own good, then gave his benediction and last-minute weather forecast for approaching storms, and Anders kindly filled me in on the intricate access through the rocky canyon gates.

Alcohol had worn thin by then, and I redressed as a twinge of doubt stuck like a bone in my throat and a tiny voice asked way back, "Do you really want to do this?" You bet, I thought, and with an adiós pushed off into the ultimate unknown, never having been alone for long on a river.

In most of the unfolded canyons, the river travels through similar-aged layers of marine limestone, but at the far end of the great Big Bend, in narrowly compressed Mariscal Canyon, the river penetrates back in time to its dark depositional heart, then flows out again to the present on the other side. I entered quietly in the late afternoon, passed irregular barriers, and found myself in a moist cathedral filled with wild-flower incense. Light fell snow-soft on smooth rocks, and a timeless patience pervaded the great hollow from which cubic miles of stone were taken, a work incomprehensible except by

being in the consequent void. The shallow river looked so innocent, yet its mercurial essence belied immense forces forever beyond our control. All at once the folded walls soared up and narrowed down to a slender corridor against the Mexican shore, where I stopped as advised, to scout, and frightened a red racer in the dry champagne grass. I went to the edge of the battered block that chokes the whole river to a passage scarcely three yards wide at the Tight Squeeze and stared in disbelief.

It looked mighty tricky, but to portage single-handed over the breakdown was impossible. I drifted on the edge to the throat, turned to barely miss Texas, then pulled hard on the left, ascended a roaring pillow, and dropped down the other side on a breathless roller-coaster ride. I whooped and hollered like a fool plunging through, only to meet a jet boat coming straight toward me. There was no way out, so I grabbed a friendly eddy. The jet boat swerved, and the captain backed down with his deadly wake, so I broke out and passed by with a look that could have killed. I was shaking hard as I landed on a sand bar to recover, and when shiny cans drifted onto the beach, I got up and stomped them flatter than they had to be.

Tossing more cans, the good buddies chugged up after quickly checking their rigs gigged into the fractured walls head high from the water line. They opened an emptied cooler and showed me the afternoon's catch. Doubled around itself, filling a twelve-gallon chest, was one tough, muddy catfish, ancient inedible witness to great floods of the past.

The Odessa sportsmen offered me a tow, but I declined in favor of staying alive. They were upset by the thought of my going alone and asked, "Ain't you scared of wild animals, accidents, bandits, or something?"

"Only your kind," I replied.

They got my drift and left in oily clouds. When the canyon fell silent, I risked traveling again, gawking at towering spires fit for falcons' aeries, but crunching rock and rippling aluminum caught my attention as the canoe scraped over submerged stone.

Tired of total awareness, I pulled out below Cross Canyon Rapids and camped on the tail of a migrating dune. The sky glazed over at sundown, the wind picked up curtains of sand, and cane bent low in stately arches.

I did not sleep much that night. Instead, I got up to chase things blown out of the boat, and although the wind dropped once in the yellow dawn, it steadily increased for two more days. In the morning, heavy clouds tore over the rim, whipped up a chilling spray, and incidentally kept the camera from standing still.

Steady gales later changed to stronger gusts that buffeted everything from river to rim. At times the wind blew so hard it pushed me back up short rapids. On the third pass at one, I decided to get out and seek shelter in the lee of broken rocks, but sand drifted out of suspension so fast I could have suffocated. Birds were unseen, but their hushed twittering came in snatches from brush by the water, and all flights were indefinitely grounded. Bored of waiting, I eventually turned backwards, straddled the stern with my knees, and pulled the whole loaded show into the wind. At white water I switched and ran naturally, then resumed a backward stance for straightaways. With that advanced program I went into sheer-walled San Vicente Canyon and rested in a deep recess. Waves three feet high rolled by as the canoe banged rhythmically, and I studied a six-foot sand spit on the other side. It was not a lot of camp, but that was all I had seen for an hour, and in cold rain with light sleet, I decided to go for it rather than sleep in a tossing boat.

I sneaked out of the overhang and hugged the Mexican cliff to the bend, then paddled like hell for Texas. A solid wall of wind tried to spin me, and waves washed in. I brought the bow around and pulled for all I was worth but just stood still. So I worked back and forth, creeping past the bar, then turned in the first lull and let a gust sweep me over to shore.

Exhausted, I dragged the canoe up as best I could and tied off, expecting floods by morning. I threw together a crude boulder camp and climbed to look around. Trails laced the rim, well defined by poachers and candelilla scalpers, so I could have walked out if the river turned impossible. I would not have perished for want of a way, only the sense to take it. I dropped back into camp for a cup of hot cocoa, then crouched through the night, since there was no room for sleep.

I ate cold, packed, and left before sunrise to evade the gales, but right away downriver cane swayed, and ghost trains whistled over the plateau. All day the pattern repeated: tack and run, then turn and tack again. I came to accept hard work and the stormy threat of drowning as normal conditions, with no other thought than survival. But when I finally cleared San Vicente Canyon, I was unexpectedly rewarded with a splendid view of April snow on the white Chisos Mountains and the Sierra del Carmen deep into Mexico.

Boquillas Canyon

I explored Boquillas Canyon in the Sierra del Carmen with David Hollingsworth on an unusual run one September as a tropical storm entered the Gulf of Mexico a thousand miles away and pumped moisture north through the Big Bend along the Sierra Madre. Showers, flies, and a bloody sunrise announced our first river day as we got cold juice and fried pies from the Stillwell Store, where Mrs. Harris wisely advised that lots of ragged clouds and clouds of biting flies are sure signs of rain. "Red skies at morning, sailors take warning." We briefly reconsidered, then let desire override better judgment.

It was all hot creosote bush, lechuguilla, and dusty bumps down to the river with a takeout truck, then back around to Rio Grande Village for the start. Cumulonimbus piled over the ranges, thunder boomed, and streamers fell around us. Drugged in the humid heat, we took hours to rig and simply ignored the storm.

"Think it might rain?" I asked as we casually slipped away. Dozens of unseen eyes watched from the green ribbon oasis of vines, tules, morning glories, and dense foreign cane. Something large slid down the Mexican beaver slide ahead of us and disappeared like a diving submarine. Driven by heat, black bears and tawny cougars also often cross the river in desperate seasons, and several had already been spotted that summer.

As we drifted past the village of Boquillas, a young man got up from the sand under his thatched jacal, walked to the edge, knelt, and drank directly from the green river. He rose as we passed, looked us in the eyes, wiped his mouth on his shirttail, then walked proudly back to his friends. Faith alone gave him immunity to any danger in that water, and lifelong drinking afforded tolerance and appetite for it. I have seen this before, I thought, but where?

David called me back to the present at the first

fault scarp by the entrance to the canyon where the Sierra del Carmen vaults above the Sunken Block of Udden and warm springs well out along offset barrier planes. Outside, the world was heavy with cold rain spilling off the Mexican mountains. We camped about a mile inside, and the wind began to blow while we cooked and ate grit in my new alpine tent. Shortly after we sacked out, gusts blew up to fifty miles an hour, and the high-tech shelter, designed to stand on the continental divide, bent absolutely flat. "I can't take much more of this," David croaked. I asked if we had any choice. "Good point," I heard him mumble, as though with a foot in his mouth.

By morning our tracks were gone, and turbulent air pummeled us without break. Another windy week, I thought, fighting white caps on the Rio Grande. But fate was with us. The storm turned downstream, and the canyon itself stepped back in enormous limestone blocks broken to the top of Pico del Carmen. Towards evening the winds eased a little, but unable to face the tent again, I stretched out on bare sand. The river threaded light between darkness and bright night sky, and long clouds trailed out of the south, opening and closing around the seductive moon.

The restless, mosquito-filled night begat a slow-going morning, and into my second pot of coffee I asked, "Why do we do this, Hollywood?"

He grinned from behind dark glasses: "Because it's so restful."

The misty land was soft lavender and pale green, and small rings spread over the river. It was evident that we might need to cut short our trip, and I agreed to go for the special of the week. We pitched our camp at Arroyo Conejos by late afternoon and then hiked into a hidden passage a few feet wide and hundreds of feet deep cut in the vertical canyon side.

Parthenogenic whiptail lizards skittered along the slick floor, unable to escape except at random breaks. Pockets of fossil soil supported high-rise communities on fluted columns that soared from weathered walls, and by streaked channels catclaw and sage clung to the massive stone trellis. Several ten-ton marbles choked the way, and at times we had to chimney up and pull gear after us.

David opted for a siesta in the first wide place, so I walked on alone through gravel trenches that crunched and rolled without much purchase. The chasm seemed endless, and I, too, tired and settled on a finite piece of bedrock. Silence surrounded me as soon as my struggle ceased, and then a glossy raven sailed by with measured flaps and studied glides, its feathers singing with each slow stroke. "Hello," I called. "Tok, tok," came back, and I followed *Corvus corax.*

Down at camp, David nursed a warm beer as he cooked. "That's a regular interstate highway," I said.

He nodded. "I noticed the scat."

Lightning flashed somewhere south of hearing, and clouds scudded low. We sat dwarfed on the tumbled outwash plain of an immense arroyo that cleaved the world at our backs. We had seen no one else for two days, and for all we knew, the entire world was ours.

Repacking my camera, I asked, "What really brings you here? What single most important thing compels you to drive halfway across flat Texas to risk your life on these overgrazed hills?"

David silently poked the stew, searching old memories and seasons spent on that land. "It may sound crazy," he finally replied, "but I guess I like it here just because it's so empty. It's a place where I can be alone, with the hermit in me, before other people have written their history on the rocks."

The Despoblado offers me an immense sanctuary in which to be alone long enough to settle and finally see the underlying truth of humanity that leads to the fact we cannot love part of life and hate the rest. It is all one body, struggling awake from the deep sleep of sentient matter, evolving out of nothing toward the light. We are no better or worse than viral molecules or the whole association of the living world, but we are blessed with the agony of knowing.

I went in again the next morning, but a brief shower flushed me out as gray clouds dragged their bellies across the Sierra del Carmen and the Dead Horse Mountains, bleeding life to the earth. Floods threatened, so we packed with thunder and left. Translucent and glowing from weeks of fair weather, the river clouded slightly at the edges, but once the ground saturated, thirsty clays swelled and sealed the earth to further entry. Sliding on mud, waters from hundreds of eroded square miles discharged directly into the river, shortcutting conventional channels, carrying nutrients from the sierras to the sea.

Daylight died, the bottom dropped out, and torrents fell at the rate of at least half a foot an hour. The boat filled with rain as we paddled on flat water, so we took shelter in a shallow cave. That was a mistake. Rivulets snaked down the walls, dislodging cannonball-sized cobbles, so we dashed out between windrows to the wallowing canoe, bailed furiously, then paddled to the middle. Still uncertain of our own future, we passed a sad cow, sunk to her hips in muddy quicksand. Not far on, a calf got the attention of *vaqueros* with lariats who pulled and pried, just ahead of the swollen flood. Thixotropic mud is firm at first touch, but with agitation the saturated sediments turn soft, and unwary waders find it impossible to get away.

We rounded a bend in our last river mile and heard rapids where none should be. From Texas, an arroyo equal in flow to one-third of the Rio Grande jumped its banks and pushed us clear to the Mexican side. Our intended landing was the mouth of a Texas arroyo, but with every one for the last five miles running wide, we stayed far right and stopped at a conservative bar. Across the turbid river a thin trickle gathered on bedrock at our take-out place. Had the runoff already ended, we wondered, or was it on its way?

We ferried upstream, crossed the main current, and turned down the center. Then with one chance at best, David grabbed an eddy on the left while I pushed hard on the right. We slammed off the bank and pulled in close, and he jumped out to tie to a well-rooted bush. Water rushed up the empty draw and got louder as we hauled to the top, but no flood appeared. We slid over shallow mud in the twilight and found the reason why behind a low earthen dam that drowned ocotillo, cactus, and mesquite. The only road out led over an old dirt bank that the water was eagerly undermining, and as David walked across, wide cracks opened. He jumped back, kicking off with one foot, and the whole span collapsed in a muddy surge.

A thick tongue lapped the arroyo, tasting every rock and low place like a serpent hunting the river, and in seconds it swelled, too wide to cross. Undercut banks crumbled, and hundred-pound boulders clanked on the bottom. For weeks flash floods disrupted travel all over the Despoblado as an upstart Pacific cold front collided with a full-blown Caribbean hurricane, and tropical rains temporarily turned the desert tender green.

Rio Grande Lower Canyons

Ironically, I took my first Big Bend river trip not at the beginning, but at the end, so to speak, through the unfolding labyrinth of the Lower Canyons. I put in one clear October morning at the mouth of Maravillas Creek with Whole Earth Travel compadres from Austin. When the rafts were inflated and rigged, shuttle drivers Tracy Lynch and David Sleeper, old desert dancers, delivered candid lectures about the proper sanitary care of a river. Most of us had never thought about what to do with processed food or waste water, but, basically, we learned to urinate well away from streams and springs and to defecate on high ground in shallow pits that can be covered to allow for soil digestion without dessication. Dedicated river rats use flat stones instead of toilet tissue, although Indian tobacco is a softer substitute. Paper does not break down for years out here, like citrus peel or instant photo wrappers, and it floats right out of loose sand. Commercial trips and groups of six or more are requested to use porta-potties to pack their wastes safely out.

We shoved off just before noon, shot the first rapid, and then eased up for a lazy lunch. Afterward, a long, tedious rhythm of meandering strokes imposed itself on our half-hearted efforts to follow the shifty currents across wide-open Outlaw Flats. Slackwater madness often overcame us in the form of giddy bucket battles that tumbled rafters overboard in the knee-deep river. "What kind of joke is this?" we asked David Hollingworth, our trip leader.

"It gets deeper, believe me," he pleaded, and so, overloaded and underfloated, we crawled on for two days before entering Reagan Gorge.

Near a huge round boulder on the sandy Mexican side we surprised a golden eagle drinking directly from the green water. It was an immature *Aquila*, clove brown, not yet crowned with the radiance of years spent soaring free above the whole, wide, desolate desert. The dapper young monarch of hawks was broad-shouldered, with feathered leggings, brilliant yellow feet, massive black talons, a slate gray bill, and dark eyes keen enough to see small rodents from a thousand yards away. The silent associate of lonely mesas watched us pass, taking everything into its avian view, then flew ahead to a polished rock and stopped. Without warning, it hurled itself from the stone, right over us, bent the air with thunderous wings, and flashed inner white primaries before climbing above the canyon walls.

Toward sundown the next day, heralded by tumultuous bleating, we reached Hot Springs Rapid at Canyon San Rosendo and encountered a disgusting scene. Hundred of goats churned the banks into dusty clouds filled with no-see-um gnats, the shore was paved with fecal pellets, and the air buzzed with sabertooth flies. We were forced to portage our gear around the exposed boulders of the low-water slide while ravenous ruminants pressed close to our brightly colored life jackets and rubber rafts. Finally, rerigged but unrested, we drifted beyond sight, smell, and sound of that desperate turmoil to an isolated arroyo downstream.

The following morning we left early, rounded Bullis Fold Bend, and pulled out to scout Palmas Rapid. No big thing, it seemed, except for the dog-leg turn between blocks of rock that split the main flow, but I carried my camera around just on a hunch. David ran clean through with Linda Howard and Will Brown. Then Andrea Wakefield, Ann Matlock, and I shoved off. Everything went fine until we hit a high roller and wrapped on a rock. Andrea washed into the current, her ankle caught in a tangled bowline, and a swift undertow kept her down. David rushed out and lifted her shoulders, and Will jumped in to cut the deadly line. Short, sawlike strokes finally freed her from disaster, but she lost her glasses and a shoe and shed a little pride.

The boat peeled off the rock, and we collected most of our gear. Then Tim Shropshire, Nancy Yarborough, and Joe Ray Jones made an all-or-nothing lunge down the hungry tongue and flipped at the very same spot. Their raft floated harmlessly out, surrounded by high-dollar flotsam. For hours and miles we collected goods and discovered that not all waterproof bags are really dry.

Thwarted by head winds, and behind schedule, we scraped through shallow pools and dragged over flat gravel bars in an extended struggle out of the canyon. Clouds gathered steadily for three days, and lightning played one night on the western horizon. At Burro Bluff rapids, we carried past dry Tule Canyon in a drizzly rain, then portaged again at Lower Madison Falls. Finally, beaten by the windy fight to San Francisco Canyon, we pitched a late camp on the Mexican side opposite an enormous empty wash.

Lightning came again, with thunder and rain just in time for dinner, as we hunkered in slickers, backs to the wind, fending sand from our food. In the feeble glare of a small flashlight, David read to us a tale of genuine horror from a letter by Jim Underwood about an old Outward Bound group bedded down solo up San Francisco's parched draw: "On 9 August at about 2 A.M. in clear starry weather a six inch riffle of water came down San Francisco Canyon, hissing across the gravel, followed in 5-10 seconds by a one or two foot bore of muddy water, all preceded by an earthquake-like roar. The bore rolled and splashed and behind, the water rose quickly to a height of six feet or more, covered with sticks and debris of all kinds, rolling and plunging in the strong current.

"Forty hours later, at 8:30 P.M., after an hour of hard local rain, a second deeper bore roared down the creek with a deafening sound, cut across the Rio Grande, and washed over the lower portion of our camp, which was actually up river from the creek mouth. The Rio Grande flowed upriver for thirty-seven minutes and rose from four feet to twelve in depth. People camped near the rim of the narrows spoke of incredible water depths in San Francisco Canyon, which we measured next day at well over 100 feet."

When David finished, we were all deathly quiet, sitting on the same bar that flood had washed over. Before stuffing into sultry tents, we scouted the cliffs for escape routes and carried gear and rafts thirty feet up to the highest part of our temporary world. Shortly after we turned in, huge gusts swept down, uprooting tents and scattering utensils. Lightning stalked around on crackling legs, and, unable to sleep, we joked nervously about the Outward Bounders.

The storm lasted till morning, and when we crawled out gritty-eyed, all we could do was stand in disbelief. San Francisco Canyon ran wall to wall, pushing muddy water into the river, driving foam back upstream. Our beach was gone, and I wandered along along the new high-water line where the evening before a lush bank lay covered with sedge and jointed horsetails.

Riding the muddy rise, swimming with rattlers

and rafts of cane, we quickly made up lost time, although the weather continued unsettled. A hazy blue sky simmered into the afternoon, and then from the southwest white anvil heads threatened. We pulled up and tied off on a long, grassy vega that rustled with furtive creatures.

We cooked and saluted to the sound of hail drumming past, then partied the last night away under limestone ledges. The brunt of the storm finally hit around midnight, sending late sots to bed, and in the morning we packed a soggy camp for an early takeout at Dudley Harrison's landing ahead of more afternoon rains. The worst downpours came shortly after we got off the river, back at Bill Teneyck's Dryden Mercantile. A friend who later flew over the flood reported San Francisco, Tule, San Rosendo, and all the shallow draws running big, with waterfalls cascading from every rim. The places we camped went completely under, and no rocks showed, even on the island at Burro Bluff—only turbulent waves standing taller than cane.

Pleistocene Ghost

I saw not only the seasons changed but also the fundamental values of the Despoblado completely reversed the last time I went to take pictures for this book. I drove alone at night to Pine Springs, through sleet and sticky snow, then slept at the National Park campground in my Land Cruiser while hundred-mile-an-hour winds whipped blizzards over the peaks and down the canyons. In morning light, the whole figure-ground of the Guadalupe Mountains was inverted. White valleys advanced, and dark boulders receded, entirely deceiving my senses.

Glazed chino grasses and maple leaves cracked like brittle china in brutal winds. Fins and ghostly pinnacles materialized and disappeared with each icy wave, and lively steam poured out of gypsum caves. Hexagonal crystals laced over shallow pools while little birds huddled in warm grassy igloos. Crickets and grasshoppers, out late, played their last hit tunes, and one slow fiddler rode out of the high country in my padded camera case only to find a skiff of snow right down on the dry salt flats.

Spiky plants looked funny with ice stuffed into every nook and cranny, but not even silly yuccas could laugh. I made a few photographs, froze my fingers and toes, then skidded backwards, out of control, fishtailing into the only ditch around. I calmed down, pulled out, and crept south to the Davis Mountains, where the frosted Sawtooth Peaks leaned together like hoary old trolls as if for warmth and protection.

Again I climbed into freezing clouds, and time ceased. There was no sun to tell direction, and only the waxing and waning of pure light marked the passing day. A late photographer friend, Laura Gilpin, once told me, "Light is the important thing. Too many people forget that, yet without shadow, there is no form. Flashes of light illuminate themselves, but it takes light and dark together to know either."

Forty-eight hours after it began, the storm ended. Warm shafts split the sky, and by evening, ice lay only in shadows. Under a clear moon, soggy ground refroze, prying stones loose, and in the morning talus cascaded from thawing escarpments as the white Pleistocene ghost faded into thin, dry air.

Arm Waving

On a grand scale, it appears the amorphous earth first acquired its crusty identity about three billion, eight hundred million years ago, long after our smaller sister moon had acquired hers. Locally, the varied Trans-Pecos landscape is covered with sand, gravel, and dust, some of which fell just today. The interval between the new and the old is full of episodic, orogenic catastrophe, erosionally interspersed with vast depositional boredom.

It may be that cooling ever so slowly, a thin shell formed that for aeons more broke and sank, remelted, and circulated, venting primal gasses and juvenile moisture sweated from young molecules deep in the earth. An infant atmosphere eventually evolved, and a rudimentary ocean precipitated, further cooling the fevered world.

About two and one-half billion years before present, the firm foundations of basement rock that had accumulated swirled and elevated into the venerable cratons, ancient heraldic shields of continental genealogy. Within half a billion more years, the lithosphere froze rigid enough to crack into mosaic plates, and from the absence of definite mountain roots much older than two billion years, it appears global tectonics may have arisen slightly before then.

For another one billion, eight hundred million years, plates were born, drifted, and fell into churning caldrons, leaving only fragments to tell of endless cycles of emergence and subduction. Driven by unexplained thermodynamic forces associated with dark interior motions of the athenosphere and upper mantle, at this moment fundamental crust wells up in ocean basins to fill hot rifts that expand as cool, dense plates pull apart downslope, to slowly plunge around the world, and to be consumed in marine trenches or under lighter continental dross. Consequently, the oldest bedrock of the deep sea floors has been there no more than two hundred million years, even though older deposits have been found, floating isostatically, on high ground.

Perhaps celestial impacts, close planetary calls, or uncertain distributional inequities wobbled the earthly egg, cracked its shell, and scattered pieces far and wide. Whatever the mechanisms, they still glide and collide, convulsively generating and destroying suboceanic surface, as the planet thrives.

Precambrian stones exposed around the Diablo Platform and in the Franklin Mountains near El Paso reveal the earliest structural systems of Trans-Pecos Texas. The Carrizo Mountain group contains the oldest rocks, with 19,000 feet of folded arkose, quartzite, schist, limestone, and rhyolite that were deformed into metamorphic ranges and eroded one and one-quarter billion years ago. The Allamoore and Hazel formations are second in seniority, consisting of 7,500 feet of limestone, dolomite, sandstone, conglomerate, and volcanic rocks that were complexly deformed and lightly metamorphosed a thousand million years ago as another mountain system was made and then erased.

A staggering unconformity of eroded rock separates the Proterozoic formations from the late Precambrian Van Horn sandstone that tilted without metamorphism in the third major regional uplift of the Despoblado shortly after the Atlantic Ocean initially opened nearly six hundred million years ago. Deposition returned in Cambrian time, as the local continental shelf submerged, and proceeded more or less uninterrupted through the Pennsylvanian period, laying down limestone, shale, novaculite, conglomerate, sandstone, and chert in the Marathon Trough hundreds of miles to the east. Then, in the fourth Trans-Pecos orogeny, more than three hundred million years back, fifteen thousand feet of compacted synclinal sediment was intensely deformed, folded, and thrust faulted into the Big Bend. This was contemporaneous with the main rise of the Appalachian Mountains and reclosure of the Proto-Atlantic Ocean as ancient continents collided. The present Pacific Basin is the diminutive descendant of the ancestral ocean, Panthalassa, which temporarily surrounded the last great landmass of Pangaea that reassembled from older wandering plates late in the Paleozoic era.

Shallow marine sandstones and platform carbonates with reef facies formed over wide areas of West Texas in the Permian Period as oceans encroached again 280 million years ago, yet abyssal turbidites settled on clastic subsea fans in the sinking Delaware Basin. Then while the Gulf of Mexico began to subside, the antecedent Chihuahuan Trough started to collect halite and gypsum where Pinto Canyon now erodes and continued to receive extensive evaporites, sporadically, through the Triassic and Jurassic periods. Once more, Pangaea splintered, the Atlantic Ocean reopened, the Big Bend lifted slightly, and the Sierra Nevada first rose as volcanic island arcs.

At the beginning of the Cretaceous period 135 million years ago, most of the Despoblado was submerged a final time beneath warm seas. Eventually over eighteen thousand feet of sandstone, shale, and massive limestone were deposited in the active Chihuahuan Trough on top of Mesozoic salt beds, but shallow-water sediments thinned eastward to only a few hundred feet. Sometime in the middle of the Cretaceous period, about 100 million years ago, as North America drifted westward through the Pacific Basin it encountered the old Farallon Plate. The mid-Atlantic ridge rifted to compensate for rotation, the whole continent uplifted, and massive compressional mountain building commenced.

In fits and starts, for more than fifty million years, the Laramide Orogeny folded and overthrust the eastward-tilting Chihuahuan Trough rocks while to the north, in contrast, the relatively stable Diablo Platform was only slightly deformed during uplift. Early igneous activity appeared with the injection of gabbroic sills into the Boquillas carbonates, all of which were later concordantly folded during the local anticlinal vaulting of Mariscal Mountain. Moderate deformation then continued through the close of the Cretaceous period and into the Tertiary period, from sixty-five to forty-five million years ago, as the young Rocky Mountains were made. Throughout the Paleocene and Eocene epochs the continent slowly wrinkled up, north-south, across westerly winds, and the great atmospheric rivers then lifted and cooled to rain or ice that fell on peaks and ridges but left downwind valleys and plains desert-dry in their wide shadows.

Following the Laramide Revolution, igneous sills, dikes, and batholiths intruded, culminating thirty million years back in extensive Oligocene uplift and volcanism as gas-charged magmas finally reached the surface and scorched the desolate West. Several Middle Cenozoic calderas erupted across the Trans-Pecos, including the Chinati, Chisos, and Davis mountains. These, and lesser vents, extruded thousands of feet of ash, lava, and welded tuffs that are still slowly weathering away. Volcanism ended in the Despoblado about sixteen million years ago after dike swarms in the Sierra Vieja and at Black Gap, with scattered basalt flows in the Bofecillos Mountains and, finally on the Diablo Plateau.

Basin-and-range block faulting further intensified volcanic relief after the Tertiary igneous activity ceased, and the western third of the continent extended forty miles while the Pacific Coast ranges uplifted. For twenty million years in the Miocene and early Pliocene, sediments shed into graben basins from rotating horst block ranges buried most of West Texas beneath a couple of miles of poorly sorted, flood-deposited sandy conglomerate.

Basins remained closed, with internal deposition and evaporite accumulation, until about two million years ago, when integration of regional drainages began to carve the great Big Bend canyons and to carry the rubble away. Pleistocene glaciers did not lie directly on the Despoblado, but small ones were as close as central New Mexico, and northern continental ice sheets indirectly affected Trans-Pecos Texas for a million years or more.

Back when Laramide uplift first blocked Pacific winds, the Big Bend turned semiarid to subhumid, but the end of the last ice age about ten thousand years ago marked the beginning of a severe drying trend that has preserved West Texas like a mummy. Mesic conditions lingered from about 7000 to 3000 B.C., then sometime nearly forty-five hundred years ago the modern xeric trend of cool, dry winters with hot, showery summers set in. A brief moist reprieve occurred between 1000 B.C. and A.D. 200, but the last seventeen hundred years have grown progressively drier.

Archaeologists and paleobotanists poking about in dusty caves have used artifacts, fossils, and pollen grains to sketch mental maps of prehistoric vegetation and animal migration. Along green paths, through muddy hollows, following the summer rounds of rain and melting ice, on the cold, windy edge, Indian ancestors wandered after roving herds and a rising flame. Even then a dim light cast flickering shadows, and old memories stirred ghosts in time's dust. Through upland grasses, under fir and spruce, people gathered wild nuts, fruits, and herbs to supplement game. By rolling rivers, under tall piñon pines, oaks and maples flowered, and tender seedlings wove water, light, and air into dark, organic soil.

Magnificent herds of giant creatures once grazed the great plains to the edge of West Texas, pursued by formidable predators, including human big game hunters, and although post-Pleistocene people did not singlehandedly do in the shaggy beasts, they forever tripped a critical balance. Armed with stone points, raging fires, and the crude trick of rational thought, they swept through forest and savanna. Then, as the meat ran out or gave up and died, they tried the encroaching desert plants and discovered alternate ways to survive.

Basic human habits have altered only slightly since the last ice age ended, yet we adapted to rapidly changing conditions by tight subsistence harmony and managed to stay alive for thousands of years. Those were not easy times, to be sure, but then at least we were each significant and responsible for ourselves instead of nameless government statistics helplessly impoverishing the earth. I do not advocate a return to Neanderthal ways; enough are in charge right now. All I seek is sympathetic recognition of our planet's prior right to life.

After all, whatever befalls us as individuals involves the whole world. From the molten core to the filtering atmosphere, all that supports us results from the intimate coevolution of animals, plants, and the wakeful planet itself.

This earth lives and breathes and weeps with us in the golden light of our sun. Astronauts, back from the dead moon with rocks and photographs, taught us that. But more than just a lively little ball with scattered forests, scorched deserts, fertile prairies, and frozen poles, it is a singular paradox, a solitary blue jewel, and the place of our long journey home.

Drought blasts the turf, but its unhealing blast to human hope is glossed over. The body's thirst for water is a recurring theme, but human thirst for love and just thinking is beyond consideration. Horses run with their rider to death or victory, but fleeting beauty haunts no soul to the "doorway of the dead." The land is often pictured as lonely, but the lone way of a human being's essential self is not for this extrovert world. The banners of individualism are carried high, but the higher individualism that grows out of long looking for meanings in the human drama is negligible. Somebody is always riding around or into a "feudal domain." Nobody at all penetrates it or penetrates democracy with the wisdom that came to Lincoln in his loneliness. "As I would not be a slave, so I would not be a master. This expresses my idea of democracy. Whatever differs from this, to the extent of the difference, is no democracy." The mountains, the caves, the forests, the deserts have had no prophets to interpret either their silences or their voices.

J. Frank Dobie

Plates

Hurricane clouds blowing through Guadalupe Pass.

Moonrise over McDonald's, from El Paso's Scenic Drive.

Dusky haze above Juárez and El Paso.

Fluted headwall of Victorio Canyon in the Sierra Diablo.

Branched flash flood arroyos eroded in Victorio Canyon.

Chisos phantoms shrouded by mist and snow.

Mountain mahogany, wild roses, and tall grasses in the Guadalupe Mountains.

Figure-ground snow on the Franklin Mountains.

Wind-feathered ice.

Snowy chutes and slides east of the Guadalupes.

Blizzard around El Capitan at Guadalupe Pass.

Chollas and gray oaks in a freezing fog.

Clouds and ice on Mount Locke in the snowbound Davis Mountains.

Snow on soap-tree yucca and walking-cane cholla.

Ice remnants on the rim rock above Pinto Canyon.

Bigtooth maples and eroded fossil mounds in a Guadalupe canyon.

Maples, oaks, pines, and limestone boulders.

Relict maples, oaks, and pines intertwined.

Snakebush, *Larrea*, and woolly foot grasses.

Dry foothills south of the Guadalupe highlands.

Summer three-awn grasses in an Alpine meadow.

North face of Baldy Peak on top of the Davis Mountains.

Uplifted Permian fossil reef at Victorio Divide in the Sierra Diablo.

Rock pile and Sawtooth Peak west of Mount Livermore.

Mexican catchfly blooming by lichened igneous boulders.

Juniper seedling and new red berries near Sawtooth Mountain.

Basketgrass, croton, and rain-soaked Marfa Plains.

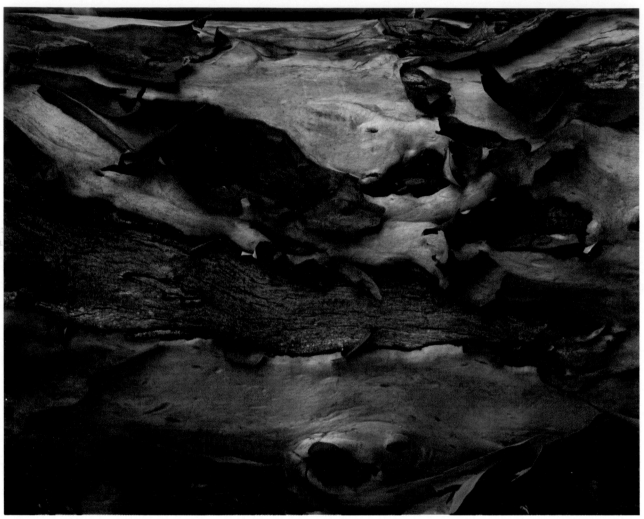

Madrone bark.

Algae in Limpia Creek near Fort Davis.

Emory Peak and Chisos Mountains brush.

Lightning-blazed alligator juniper.

Cardinal flowers, maidenhair fern, and tules by slick rocks.

Maples, oaks, Arizona cypress, and weeping juniper in a high-country canyon.

Polished stone at the Basin Window pour-off.

Bigtooth maple leaves on still water.

Mescal agave, snakebush, and prickly pear in the Chisos Basin.

Mariola, lechuguilla, and strawberry pitaya by the Grapevine Hills.

Sunrise from the South Rim of the Chisos Mountains.

Obsidian waters and autumn leaves.

Sunrise on dry grasses near Cerro Castolan.

West face of the Chisos Mountains.

Mineralized slickensides on a fault face.

Sotol and *Notholaena* star fern in a pocket of igneous soil.

Evening storm over Hueco domes.

Morning clouds around the Hueco Mountains.

Red rain near Candelaria.

Pebbles and mud cracks by the Rio Grande.

Capote Falls.

Springs in the Sierra Vieja.

Cottonwoods, willows, and New Deal weed.

Poisonous baileya on Rio Grande floodplains.

Lechuguilla and dry chino grass.

Volcanic tinaja below Burro Mesa.

Colorado Canyon and the Rio Grande.

Tree tobacco and mesquite in Fresno Canyon.

Hoodoo demoiselles near El Polvo.

Salt cedars in Colorado Canyon.

Rio Grande at the upstream entrance to Santa Elena Canyon.

Upper Barrier at the Santa Elena Rock Slide.

Boulders and reflections.

Collapsed cliff at the Rock Slide.

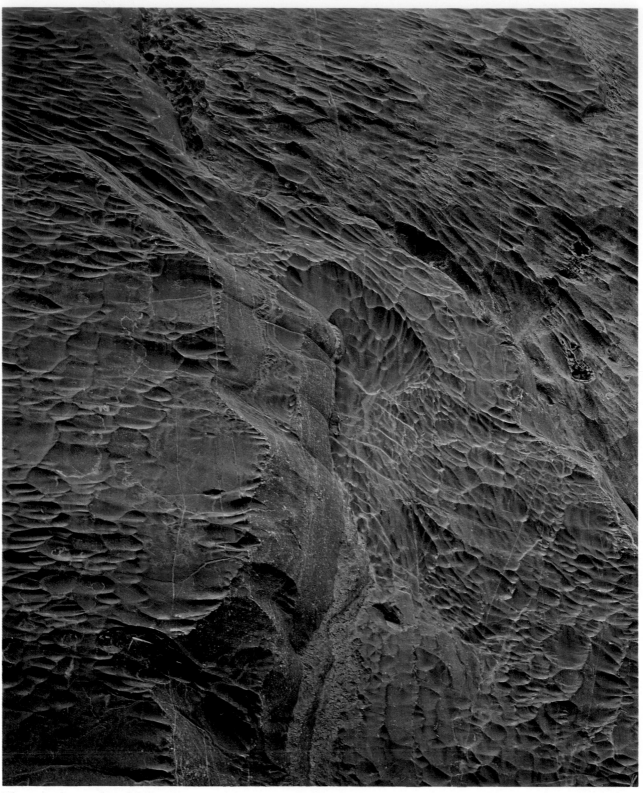

Flow marks on fluted limestone.

Dawn at the mouth of Santa Elena Canyon.

Igneous sills and low eroded lands by the Rio Grande.

Candelilla wax plants at Glenn Springs.

River cane and grapevines near Boquillas Village.

Fluffgrass, dead ocotillo, and desert pavement around Tally.

Mariscal Canyon above the Tight Squeeze on the Rio Grande.

Flood-carved iceberg rock.

Sand blowing around polished boulders.

April dust storm at the Mariscal cross-canyon.

Water- and wind-eroded sandstone.

J. O. Langford's Rio Grande hot springs.

Ash and lava remnants on the Sunken Block of Udden.

Dying pool by salt-encrusted Tornillo Creek.

Convolutions in a Sierra del Carmen arroyo.

Pico del Carmen, above Boquillas Canyon and the Rio Grande.

Rock nettles.

Sandburs and Big Bend bluebonnets.

Dry coyotillo and emerging yucca flowers.

Sandbar and reflected boulders above San Francisco Canyon.

River cave in the Rio Grande Lower Canyons.

Pools and polished rock.

Mineral-stained box canyon walls.

White rocks, blackbrush, and huisache.

Whitewater rapids at Burro Bluff on the Rio Grande.

Devil-weed, Bermuda grass, and shallow-water riffles.

Madison Falls below Burro Bluff.

Ocotillo and pitaya on the rim of the Sierra del Burro.

Mexican buckeye and invading cane.

Grass, sedge, and horsetails after flash floods.

Desert scrub and steamy river willows near Langtry.

Acacias, blackbrush, and goat-grazed hills close to Eagle Nest Canyon.

Blue norther storming the Marathon Basin.

The drowned confluence of the Rio Pecos and the Rio Grande.

Comanche moon.